Southwest on the A303

A Novella

By

Adam Gary

For Uncle Ken

Contents

Chapter One

UNCLE BILL

My mum's arm wrapped around me and she asked if I needed anything. 'No thanks,' I said, sitting blankly on the side of my bed.

'Why don't you go out? Isn't Harry around?' she asked gently, sitting down next to me. I shook my head; there wasn't much to do these days, and everything was a drag. 'Well, I'll do something with you?' Mum pestered. I appreciated the effort, but I was very content with staying in my room reading, or watching television. The truth is, I didn't find anything in life exciting anymore, and that wasn't because my uncle had just passed away.

I remember the moment I got the news. I remember it so vividly in fact it still keeps me up at night as I relive it over and over; being forced to feel that dark, sinking feeling again, and again, completely overshadowing how I felt when I tried to remind myself of the good times.

I'd say I had a unique relationship with Uncle Bill. Technically he wasn't my uncle, he was actually my second cousin, but this was so much easier. I looked up to him like a father, and I had the utmost respect for him. He was everything I so desperately wanted to be. Smart, collected, calm, and talented beyond belief. An amazing guitar player and bassist lucky enough to grow up through the sixties and seventies.

He used to run security for music venues, and the stories he would tell me about him and his faithful guard dog Rambo were just insane.

How he had threatened to lock Ronnie Wood in the Hammersmith Odeon one night after a Bo Diddly concert, because Ronnie had been partying past curfew. Or how he had set up stage for Jimi Hendrix in a small pub in Hounslow, before Hendrix became Hendrix. 'Once we finished setting up,' he said, 'We just pissed off to the pub. To us he was just another guitar player at the time,' so casual about the whole thing. 'If only I had stuck around.' The truth is Bill was full of stories like that, some of which I'm not even allowed to mention.

One of my favourite memories of our time together came in the winter of 2011. I was nineteen years old, and didn't really know what I was doing in life. I just knew that I wanted to create, and to be an actor on the stage - which my uncle supported whole heartedly by the way - and I certainly hadn't discovered any individuality within myself. I had an idea of what I liked, and who I wanted to be, but no clue how to get there. Uncle Bill invited me to go spend some time with him and soul search.

I boarded the train from Reading to Par, a quiet town in Cornwall, excited to spend the next week and a half relaxing, hanging out with Bill, and just being away from the city. We had of course spoken on the phone for a week previously to organise the logistics and such, when Bill drifted off into one of his great stories. He was telling me about his time as a kid growing up in Chiswick, running around mischievously, and then racing back home to watch his favourite television programme, 'Quatermass,' which of course I now had to watch!

When I finally got to his bungalow in Par, I made my way inside; and in the middle of his living room sat two plastic boxes filled to the brim with films like, 'Creature from the Black Lagoon', and 'Dracula'. Monroe films, Brando films, Dean films, you name it he had it. Heaven.

By the end of that week and a half I had seen my first Brando film and had been introduced to both James Dean and Marilyn Monroe. In fact, not only had I been introduced to them, I had seen their entire collection of work. And of course the mighty 'Qautermass,' didn't disappoint either. On top of all those films, he had recorded hours upon hours of music documentaries off the television from BBC 4. I had also been introduced to his music collection, which included Peter Green's Fleetwood Mac; all the while sharing a few Jack Daniels and Coke together. Needless to say, that week and a half changed my life, and I left feeling I had found my path.

So you can imagine how I felt when I received the news last week that Uncle Bill had passed away. It had come so suddenly and hit me with a terrible force. Mum's been on the phone constantly, notifying family, and making funeral arrangements; whilst I've been unable to do much but sit in my room, desperately trying to relive that golden week. I helped mum out where I could with certain information, including getting an oversized urn which Bill had previously expressed he wanted, in order to mix his ashes with Rambo's.

Bill was a lone wolf and I have a feeling that if he had his way, he wouldn't even bother with a funeral. He'd probably be happy to drift away silently, sliding into obscurity as if he hadn't even graced the earth with his presence. He couldn't stand attention; unless it was coming from the opposite sex, then he would be as smooth as Don Juan himself.

I continued to sit on the side of my bed as my little West Highland Terrier looked up at me from the floor with her sweet, big innocent brown eyes. I gave her a pat on the head and smiled. She obviously saw this as an invitation to leap up onto the bed beside me and lay down, tucking herself up and quickly falling asleep, as she usually did.

In a few hours Mum was expecting Bill's lawyer round to go through the will with us and discuss formalities. It's funny isn't it, that men in suits can find ways to slime into your life, charging for their services, no matter what the circumstance. Damn humans have complicated life.

I wasn't entirely sure whether I was ready to go through his last wishes just yet. Maybe it's because I wanted to forget the fact that he had left us, or maybe it was because it would feel like he hadn't left us at all!

I guess I wasn't really sure what I wanted to feel. Still, time waits for no man and sure enough the afternoon came quickly; followed shortly with a knock on our door.

He was actually a really kind gentleman, sensitive to how we were feeling and approached his work slowly; and with great care. A few hours went by and I learnt that I had pretty much been left with everything, including his bungalow and was given the keys to the door on the spot. Just like that. The lawyer got to his feet, wished us well and left.

***

Days went by and Mum had made all the arrangements for the funeral, which was to take place in Par two weeks from now, and had somehow managed to contact all of Bill's friends; some of which he hadn't seen for more than eight years.

'Alex!' I heard her cry. 'Alex, get out here, quick.' I jumped up thinking something terrible had happened and raced into the living room. Out of the window I could see an old but shiny, light olive green, Volkswagen camper van being lowered from a tow truck and onto the side of the street. 'What's that doing here?' I asked, surprised to see it in London, and not parked on Bill's driveway down in Cornwall.

Apparently he had requested one of his neighbours to have it delivered to me within his will. A rough, dirty looking mechanic approached the door and asked me to sign for the van - of course I obliged - before he disappeared off down the road and into his truck, presumably heading back to Cornwall.

I walked out onto the side of the road and looked the van over. Bill had always kept good care of it as it was a passion of his. The van was a Brazilian import of the old 'VW' campers, and was the closest he could get to the ones Volkswagen made back in the seventies. He used to own one back then and of course had many stories to go along with it, some of them being hilariously explicit, which resulted in his friends nicknaming him Tinkler.

After I had a good look around the outside, I noticed there was an envelope sitting on the driver's seat. Curious, I unlocked the van and pulled it out. Quickly opening it, there was a letter tucked inside on a small piece of notepad paper.

'This story's on me.'

I stood frozen a moment. I was confused and didn't know what to make of the note. I felt my insides swirl. I looked up at the van, which sat in all her beautiful glory and turned back as my Mum peered out of the doorway. 'Come inside, I have something to give you,' she said excitedly, with a smile on her face as if she had planned this whole thing out with Bill in advance.

I walked back inside, clutching the note and sat down on the sofa, dumbstruck, with my mum next to me. 'What's this?' I asked innocently, as she handed me yet another envelope.

'It's from Bill,' she said, with a sweet look in her eyes, eager for me to open the letter. I looked out of the window as the van silently sat on the street, then gently ripped open the envelope.

'Alex,

I'd like to take this time to let you know how I feel. You know I find it hard to express myself, but you should know that I think you're alright. It's been nice getting to know you, though it was later in life – we made the best of it. We're both very alike, you and me, you know that? But you're a man now, and you need to pull yourself together, alright? Stop moping about alone in your room, feeling sorry for yourself and day dreaming all the time. Go enjoy the world. You'll get no pity from me. If you want stories of your own then you need to venture out. Keep up the hard work with your acting, I reckon you've got what it takes. Get to America and say hi to Marilyn for me,

Bill.'

I sat stunned for a moment. 'You have two weeks until the funeral,' came my mother.

'What do you mean?'

'Take the van and drive down to Cornwall, meet us there,' she replied with a gentle, nudging smile.

'I-' was all I could muster. It all came on me a bit too quick and I didn't know what to say.

'You need to get out the house, Alex. I'm fed up seeing you so miserable all the time. You've got two weeks to take the van and do what you like. Just make sure you get to the funeral.'

'But I don't even know what I'd do,' I countered, desperately trying to find a way out. The truth is, I'd feel far more comfortable sitting in my room until the day of the funeral; then just driving down there the night before. 'I don't have the money,' suddenly grasping at the financial burden of such a trip.

'Your dad and I will help out where we can. Stop looking for excuses and just go,' she generously offered. 'Just worry about getting there safely - and on time.'

I sat staring at the van, a faint sense of excitement bubbling in my stomach. I didn't have the foggiest idea what to do. Eventually I got up and made for my room. I stood for a moment, staring at the two of Bill's notes, before an uproar of adrenaline struck me and I decided that I was going to do this! I packed a few outfits and the travelling essentials, before quickly shoving it into a large camping backpack that I had bought years ago - in the hopes I would take up camping. I picked up an A-Z map, phone charger, and a few good books.

I felt anxious, but pumped. I was about to take Bill's old camper down to Cornwall, and I had no idea what I'd do when I got there. All I knew was that I was going to take the famous A303 that Bill always spoke about and enjoyed driving whenever he visited us.

And just like that, I slung the backpack over my shoulder, cuddled my Mum and dog farewell, yanked up the keys to the van, and set off in search of the nearest petrol station.

Chapter Two

ON THE ROAD

I stalled the van a bunch of times. It had this strange foreign gearbox that wouldn't allow me to get into first unless I had come to a complete stop. Bill had warned me about it plenty of times but I couldn't help myself, I already had my bad driving habits well ingrained into my brain.

It was strange. Every time I stalled, I could see Bill laughing at me in the rear view mirror with that old, 'I told you so,' look on his face, as he sat on the sofa smoking his cigarettes and drinking from a small tumbler glass with Jack Daniel's poured into it; grinning through his grey goatee. I laughed to myself at the thought of Bill watching me now, desperately shoving the gear shaft into place, cursing and restarting the engine every time I had to slow down or stop.

Finally I managed to get into a petrol station and fill up the tank. Mum had put a couple hundred pounds into my bank account, which should easily last me. I also picked up a coffee, just to keep me going.

The girl behind the counter was cute, a girl next door type. She gave me a lasting smile and wished me well. I nodded in appreciation and returned a grin, before swivelling round awkwardly, heading outside and climbing back into the driver's seat.

I started the ignition, strapped in my seatbelt and put her into first gear. 'What the bloody 'ell was that?' I heard Bill's voice jokingly scream inside my head, with that cockney accent of his. 'The girls love this van! You should be taking advantage of it!'

'Oh, shut up you old git!' I said aloud, as I looked back and saw him laughing yet again at my misfortune, with a cigarette dangling from his mouth.

'You got a lot to learn, boy!'

I squeezed down on the accelerator and headed for the M3.

Not much happened whilst on the motorway. The sky had greyed and a faint patter of raindrops hit the windscreen. Still, there was an epic sense of adventure lingering in my stomach. I had spent a long time watching Bill drive this beauty, and longed to be in the driver's seat; now here I was, driving the roads he would have driven, and listening to the beautiful purr of the mighty engine amongst the metallic framework as I went along the smooth tarmac that would take me over two hundred miles across the country.

I left the M3 at junction eight and was about to finally hit the famous A303 that would take me straight to Cornwall - almost. Fourteen miles to Andover, twenty-nine to Salisbury, and a hundred and seventeen to Exeter. I smiled as I passed the mileage sign, I was on my way. Slowly the van hummed round a bend, under the M3 and before I knew it, I was on the A303. No grand welcoming arch, or even a sign saying, 'Welcome to the historic 'A' road.' Nope, nothing grand about it at all. It was all rather anticlimactic really, but nevertheless I held the road in great regard.

It wasn't long before I passed the first 'Little Chef' roadside cafe, which always brought back great childhood memories. My dad used to take me to one as a kid for a day out. It was only down the road from us, and in those days going to the 'Little Chef' seemed like a huge adventure, filled with excitement and wonder. Those were the days. I drove passed it with a grin on my face, and a slight nod in memory of those times.

The road just seemed to go on and on in a smooth, straight line, with the most phenomenally rich greenery on either side. Trees of different sizes. Some tall, some small. Some thick and some skinny. Bushes with little sparks of yellow and white blooms upon them, and a patch of grass separating me from the oncoming traffic with yellow dandelions poking out from the ground. The sun had quickly pushed through the grey clouds and suddenly a blue sky appeared above me, such is the English weather. One minute you're driving through a hail storm, the next you're taking off your jumper and rolling down the windows. This was a comfortable heat though, no rolling down of any windows or taking off my top.

I drove straight for some time. Just me, my thoughts and the road. I soon found myself passing Andover, as evening began to draw in. There was no way I was going to make Par by tonight, I still had well over two hundred miles to go. I guess I was too excited and eager to realise at the time of leaving that this was in fact an eight hour journey and I would probably have been better off staying home, then setting out early tomorrow morning.

Despite this, I decided that I'd stop over at the next services and grab some food, a coffee and maybe an hours nap, then soldier on through the night; and that would be my adventure!

I quickly found myself driving past a brown road sign for the Museum of Army Flying and Danbury Hillfort. For a long time I've always wanted to drive onto a motorway and spend the day visiting random tourist attractions; which were pointed out by large brown road signs in the U.K. Sadly this was not that day; besides it was too late in the day now, even if I wanted to.

My eyes were getting heavier and heavier, and the more I thought about stopping off for food, the more I craved it. Typically it seemed like the next service station would never come. Eventually, after passing I don't know how many parking lay-bys with no signs for 'services', I approached Amesbury. I decided to pull off and try to find a McDonalds or something. What I found was so much more! I'd never heard of Amesbury before, and had no idea what to expect. Thankfully I let go of my anxieties and drove into the unknown.

After driving through what I first assumed to be a business park, over roundabouts and past a barren warehouse-looking building - which actually turned out to be a hotel - further down I had struck gold! A 'Toby Carvery', 'Costa Coffee', 'McDonalds' and 'KFC', 'Pizza Hut', 'Harvester' and a 'Texaco'. What luck!

I decided to go for the typical 'McDonalds', as it seemed to have the most parking spots. I parked up facing the restaurant, which featured huge windows and I immediately noticed the gaze of a young girl, who was sitting on a stool at the window, sipping on her drink through its straw. I climbed down out of the van and awkwardly walked up to the entrance, trying desperately to escape her stare.

It seemed like it took forever to get from the van to the entrance. I felt her heavy gaze weighing on me, and I felt embarrassed and awkward. Despite that though, I couldn't help but attempt a glance at her as often as I felt was respectably possible.

She was so strikingly beautiful. She had thick and vibrant red hair, which had tasseled into dread locks in places, though not all over. Her eyes pierced from her face with black eyeliner, which happened to be the only make up that she wore. She had on a men's olive green jumper, which hung from her body in just the right way. I tried a smile, but she did not return it, she just kept on staring, and sipping.

When I finally entered McDs it was very stuffy. There was a queue, but it was bearable. I waited in line for a few moments, but deep inside I badly wanted to glance back at this beautiful young woman. I began to feel anxious as I didn't want to make it so obvious, so I quickly pretended to crack my neck, then my back and in doing so looked back to where I had seen her sitting, but she'd gone.

I felt gutted, like I had lost someone I had known for some time. Of course, I'd never seen this girl before but she looked like the type of girl I had always wanted to meet. Talk about projection. I shrugged it off and finally made my order, large quarter pounder meal, before heading back out to the van.

I placed my drink on the roof, and swung open the sliding side door before reclaiming my coke and climbed up into the cosy seating area. I threw off my shoes and put my feet up. Pulled out my burger and prepared to take a bite.

Just as I raised it to my mouth a gentle Welsh voice came from the opened gap left by the bolted sliding door. 'Nice van.' I turned and there stood the glowing and radiant girl with red dreads. She smiled gently before leaning inside the opened door. She now had on a cosy parker jacket and wore sunglasses, despite the fact stars were beginning to seep through into the ever darkening sky.

I looked at her with my mouth wide open, and a greasy burger in my hands. 'Thanks,' I replied awkwardly, quickly re-boxing my burger.

'It's fine, you can eat that,' she smirked.

'Right, yeah,' I replied, fumbling the burger back out and finally tucking into it.

'Mind if I join you?' she asked, seemingly sweeter and more striking the longer she stood in front of me. 'I'll share if you will,' as she pulled out a litre bottle of rum.

'Uh-' I hesitated, 'Yeah, okay.' I said, as I clambered around. 'I'm not really here for very long, and I'm driving so I can't drink.'

'You can have one, I'm sure,' she replied, stepping up, immediately opening the cupboards under the sink. She pulled out two mugs, one of which had a yellow sticky note attached. 'For alcohol consumption only,' she read aloud, 'Interesting.'

'Oh, that's probably my uncle. I don't write notes to myself or anything,' I explained, nervously. She playfully stuck the sticky note onto her stomach, and started pouring out mugs of rum. 'That's enough!' I cried, as the rum flowed freely, but she didn't listen. Finally she turned with the cheekiest of smiles on her face and shrugged her shoulders before sitting down on the sofa next to me.

'Amy,' she said as she offered a hand out. I quickly finished off my burger and shook it with a crumb infested hand.

'Sorry. I'm Alex.'

'Nice to meet you. Great ride, how'd you get hold of it?' she asked as she inspected it with great affection.

'It was my uncles. He's, uhm, just passed away and left it to me.'

'Ah, bummer. I'm sorry,' she said with great, calming affection. My stomach began to feel light, and a little queasy. Surprisingly not due to the McDonalds I was now finishing off, but I just felt a bizarre connection with her. Her lips moved, but I wasn't taking in anything she was saying. I just kept thinking about how beautiful she was, and how I'd wished I'd met her under better circumstances.

'Well?' she asked.

'Huh?'

'Where are you off to?'

'Oh,' I fumbled quickly, trying to appear present, 'I'm heading down to Cornwall for the funeral. My uncle wanted me to have an adventure type of thing, so I'm going to drive down through the night,' I explained, attempting to be suave and cool, confident that I had impressed her. There was an awkward pause as she looked at me.

'That's your adventure?' she finally asked, looking totally unimpressed. I felt deflated, and stupid. She downed her drink, got up and began pouring herself another mug of rum. 'Finish up, I'll show you an adventure.' I felt awkward, I really didn't want to drink and drive. 'Come on man, don't you want to respect your uncle's wish properly? You're in a camper for fuck sake, you can sleep the alcohol off later.'

I looked at her a moment, 'Right,' and downed my mug of rum, 'But only a couple.' She chuckled and poured me another large mug of straight rum. We spoke for some time, and she shared with me her travel stories. She was quite the free spirit, but definitely not in a hippy kind of way. Something about her energy was dark and mischievous, but if you looked at her she appeared sweet and innocent. Perhaps that's what I liked about her so much.

She told me she had made her way from Cardiff to London, then hitch-hiked a ride here in order to get to Stonehenge for the summer solstice, which was to take place tomorrow. 'So you're a druid?' I asked.

'No not really. I just connect with the world you know, and I like a good party. I'm meeting some friends who are though, in the coolest kind of way,' she explained as she took a large gulp of her rum. The night sky was now completely black; and the car park, along with the oversized 'm' above McDonalds ignited around us.

'So seriously, what's your plan for this big adventure?'

'Well, I was just going to drive through the night, on the A303 to Cornwall. That was pretty much it.' I said, downtrodden. She looked at me shaking her head, then reached into her parker and pulled out a map.

'Lets plan out a proper adventure for you,' she said scoffing down another gulp of rum. She stood up excitably and laid the map out across the counter; taking out a red marker. I sat admiring her for a brief second, her excitable demeanour, before joining her at the map.

'Right,' she started, 'First you'll take me to Stonehenge, meet my friends and enjoy the solstice with us,' she looked at me with an inviting gaze. 'What have you always wanted to do?'

'Uhm, I'm not sure. I've always wanted to hit the motorway and visit the first brown sign I come to.'

'Good! After the solstice you'll do that. Then you'll get back on the A303 until you connect to the A30 and reach Honiton. Right?' she turned and looked at me with an excited gaze, then back to the map, marking the route with her thick red marker. 'At Honiton you'll jump to the A375 and spend some time in the "East Devon Area of Outstanding Natural Beauty", that sounds fun! From there you'll head for the A3052, towards Exeter; then you'll spend some time in there, too. Once you're finished, continue down through Longdown and drive straight through Dartmoor National park. Spend some time at Bovey Castle, then back down through to Yelverton. Jump on the A386 towards Plymouth, then A38 towards Saltash. At Dobwalls, join the A390 to Lostwithiel. Then hey presto, you're in Cornwall!' She circled 'Lostwithiel' and dotted the marker onto the map, with an excited grin on her face. 'Sound good?' she asked.

'Sounds perfect,' I replied, 'Man-' I started, but quickly caught myself.

'What?'

'You're just... awesome,' I concluded, though I wanted to say so much more.

'I know. Now, what I forgot to mention is that your adventure starts tonight. Getting drunk with me.' We had already finished half the bottle of rum by this point, and I had started to feel its effects slightly. I was good at handling my drink, and I could already see she was too. 'Don't worry, I'll try not to embarrass you too much by drinking you under the table. There's a bar in the Holiday Inn, and it's where I'm staying. Come on.'

We stepped out of the van, and just as I was stepping down, in the rear view mirror I caught a glimpse of Uncle Bill giving me an approving thumbs up. I smiled and left the van. I locked her up safe and sound for the night and we walked down to the hotel. We made our way inside and greeted the receptionist with a smile before heading into the bar. It was basic, but welcoming, as I imagine they all are, and we pulled up two stalls stools that sat in front of the counter.

It was relatively empty, and the older barman served us immediately. Amy ordered us four shots of tequila and two rum and cokes. 'This one's on you, in return for my amazing planning skills,' she playfully joked. I smiled at her and found my body leaning towards her slightly. The sudden urge to just be nearer to her.

The barman laid down the drinks in front of us and I settled the bill. Amy and I spent the entire night laughing and joking, as the drinks poured in. We laughed together and flirted from time to time.

We were both starting to feel rather tipsy when a man dressed in a long black trench coat walked in. He looked very serious with a constant furrowed brow, and carried a heavy leather briefcase, which he slammed onto the bar before ordering his drink. We decided to play a game where we had to guess the backstory for this particular gentleman. 'He's the head of MI5,' Amy started, 'and has traveled here under strict order of the Queen to make sure that you are having a fabulous time,' Amy slurred. I smiled.

'He's a hitman. On the hunt for his latest victim, a contract he acquired many years ago but his target is too elusive,' I countered.

'Ooh, that's good,' she said excitably.

The night went on, and early morning welcomed us. 'I'm afraid we're closing now,' came the elderly barman. We laughed and downed the remaining dregs of our drink, got to our feet and staggered into the reception area. 'It's been lovely meeting you.' I said, swaying.

'Easy tiger, we agreed you were to come to the solstice, 'member?' Amy slurred.

'Then I'll see you in the morning. Goodnight,' I replied, with a tender kiss on her forehead, before realising what I had just done with new found drunken confidence. She smiled, and I happily returned it before turning and making for the exit.

'Alex…' came Amy's voice. I turned and saw her walking towards me. 'I, uh, I don't actually have a room here. I just said that to get you in,' she continued, blushing slightly, 'Don't suppose you have room for one more in that van of yours, do you?'

I stood frozen a moment, as our eyes locked, 'Yeah.' I wrapped my arm over her shoulder, and I felt hers clutch my waist. With the fuzziest warm feeling inside I lead her outside, and we both staggered over to the van together, smiling from ear to ear.

We clambered into the van, and I pulled out the bed from under the sofa. Another sticky note fell out, and I quickly grasped it.

'I hope you're pulling this out with a bird next to you, and not with the intention of pleasing yourself. Either way you're a lucky git, I've not been able to do either for years.'

I smiled to myself and scrunched up the note, lobbing it to the side. 'Do I want to know?' came Amy's voice. I looked over and was rendered stunned. Amy had stripped down to her underwear and had pulled out the pillows and duvet, making the bed. Her figure was out of this world, and I was lost for words. The moonlight reflected off her skin perfectly. She was such a magnificently carefree creature. I smiled, shook my head and pulled the window curtains shut before taking off my top. I climbed into bed and we spent a beautifully spontaneous night of passion together.

Chapter Three

STONEHENGE

I awoke to the sounds of gentle rain tapping against the roof and windscreen. My head ached, and my surroundings swayed. The scent of strawberries invaded the air as Amy's head lay against my chest. I looked down at her and she appeared completely at peace with the world. I smiled to myself and watched her a while. For a brief moment, life was good.

Eventually she stirred from her slumber, and looked up at me through glazed eyes. She smiled sweetly at me, and playfully slapped her palm on my bare chest, 'Stop it.'

'Stop what?'

'Looking at me like you're getting messy, complicated feelings.' She winked at me, and all I could do was look at her, unsure what to say. I had been developing feelings the moment I laid eyes upon her. She must have sensed this, as she quickly pulled herself out of bed, threw on her clothing - including her sunglasses - and made her way to the door. 'I'll be back in a sec, don't go anywhere.'

She rolled open the door, and stepped out, slamming it shut with a thunderous thud that shook the inside of my head as if I had just been smacked with a brick. I felt ridiculous. I wasn't used to female attention, especially from one so perfect, and my projections and silly romantic heart had made me fall for this girl in less than twenty-four hours.

I rubbed my face and braved the approaching morning by sitting up onto the side of the bed. The place spun, as if I was on one of those roundabouts you get in children's parks, going at a furious speed. I composed myself and got to my feet, pulling on my clothes. I opened the curtains and folded away the bed.

I rinsed out the mugs, popped the kettle on and opened the sliding door. The sky was dim and grey. The fresh air was awakening and a welcomed refresher as the air inside the van had become stale overnight and it was a relief to feel the cold air strike my face. After the kettle finally boiled and I prepared two black coffees, I sat down on the step between the frame of the open door and observed cars as they pulled into the services.

Eventually Amy came skipping back from the direction of the Holiday Inn, with a Co-Op plastic bag in her hand. She was relishing the gentle, drizzling rain that fell down on her. She had a massive grin on her face, spinning in circles embracing life without a care in the world. I admired her, and raised my mug in toast. She smiled and came bounding over to the van.

'Here, I got us some sandwiches for breakfast and lunch, and a chocolate bar each. I didn't know what you like so I just picked up anything,' she said, and she squeezed past me, climbing up into the van.

'Very thoughtful,' I said, though the truth is I neither liked the sandwich, nor the chocolate. It was chocolate and nuts, and that just doesn't go together if you were to ask my opinion. I got up and joined her on the couch. 'I don't have a towel or anything,' I explained.

'Ah don't worry, I got a spare top in my bag,' she said as she reached into her backpack and pulled out an oversized chequered buttoned shirt, and slung off her jeans before digging into her sandwich.

'What about your jeans?' I asked, bashful.

'They'll just have to dry. You don't mind me sitting here in my Batman knickers do you?' she asked smirking with that cheeky tone again.

'No.'

We finished our breakfasts and each splashed our faces with the water from the sink, 'What time does your solstice start?' I asked, as we both climbed into the two front seats.

'It's an all day type thing, that goes on into the night. Tom and Susan are probably already there.'

'Okay,' I replied, feeling apprehensive and anxious about attending this thing. I threw in the keys and started her up. Amy threw open the glove compartment and picked out a CD, sliding it into the stereo. Peter Green's wailing guitar on 'Supernatural' started up, singing as if just for us.

'I love this song!' she cried, looking over at me. I couldn't believe what I was hearing. I'd never met anyone who'd ever heard of Peter Green, let alone enjoy his music as much as I did. I looked over as she unwound the window and stuck her head out, laughing joyously as the rain gently tapped down onto her head.

'She's a keeper!' came Bill, from the rear view mirror. I smiled and pulled out of the car park, heading back to the A303. As we reached the road, Amy suddenly pulled her head back inside the camper and rustled her head from side to side, whipping her dreads and splashing me with excess rain water. I whipped my somewhat wet hair back, with less amusing effect.

'Oh man! It's going to be a good day,' she said excitably, before suddenly pulling her t-shirt up over her head and reaching behind to undo her bra.

'What are you doing?' I cried, suddenly looking over at her, almost veering off onto the grass and into the hedges that lined the A303.

'Jheez!' she wailed as I quickly steered us back onto the tarmac. 'I'm getting the girls out. Don't you like them?' she asked, looking down inspecting her still covered cleavage.

'Put your top back on. People might report us to the police.'

'Oh come on-'

'Please!'

'Fine,' as she threw her top back on and sulked, looking out the window. 'You worry way too much.'

Thankfully Stonehenge wasn't too far up the road and we got there quickly enough, before the awkward silence became too unbearable. It was a bit of a struggle finding the official Stonehenge parking, and Amy had heard of a place we could park for free; but she wasn't entirely sure where it was or whether it was legal.

When I pulled up, there was a steward in high visibility to welcome us. The parking charge was fifty pounds. I looked to Amy and explained I didn't have that kind of money to spend on parking. 'That sucks. I guess I can just get out here then,' she said as she reached down and threw her bag onto her lap. 'But make sure you stick to my planned route, okay?' before kissing me on the cheek.

'Screw it,' I said reaching into my pocket and pulling out my wallet and fifty pounds in notes. 'What am I doing?' I asked myself aloud, though I felt a smile creep across my face in excitement.

'Living free,' replied Amy as she tapped her hands onto the roof of the van drumming repeatedly and making a rumbling of thuds as we settled our parking bill and found ourselves a bay. It was ten in the morning, and there wasn't a great deal of cars parked, save one or two.

The rain had stopped but the sky remained grey, as the sun slowly burned away at the cloud. Suddenly a robed couple walked past, waving as they went. They looked incredibly happy. The male had on a long white robe, and smiled behind a big brown bushy beard. His lady clothed in a dark moss green gown, with some sort of twigged headdress. I returned the smile and looked to Amy. 'Let's go,' she said with great excitement.

We jumped out from the van and the fresh cold air hit us with refreshing relief. I took a deep breath and looked around. Amy took my hand and lead me through and up into the surrounding fields of Stonehenge. That light butterfly feeling returned as I felt her soft, gentle hand clasped in mine.

The grass was wet and began to soak through my shoes, into my socks and onto my feet. 'My shoes are going to be wrecked,' I complained, looking down at them, as they squelched in the glistening rain swamped grass.

'Take them off,' she said as she reached down and yanked off her own shoes and socks, before shoving them into her bag and continuing on bare foot; running on ahead with her arms outstretched, and 'Wooing' into the wind. We walked into the vast fields and up to the giant druidic stones. They took my breath away, and scattered around them were small pockets of people. I'd say no more than twenty. The majority had large beards and long hair. Some wore traditional robes and gowns, with druidic necklaces around their necks, and others were in modern dress. Some were barefoot. Amy and I searched around for her friends Susan and Tom, but it appeared they had not arrived yet, so instead we decided to admire these ancient rocks until they had appeared.

The day went on and into the early evening, with no sign of Tom or Susan. Amy and I had spent the entire day walking the vast beautiful fields surrounding the stones, greeting people and making up backstories for them. We returned to the van a few times and ate the lunches that she had picked up back in Amesbury.

We eventually made our way back over to the rocks, as the sun showed an inkling of its setting, around seven in the evening. A British summer evening is one of the most relaxing, beautiful spectacles that this land has to offer, and here I was, standing in vast open fields without a single concrete building in sight. The sky clear and blue, rich green grass and people that hadn't a care in the world.

We looked for Tom and Susan again, through the slowly growing crowd, but still no sign of them. Music had begun playing, with horns blowing and drums beating. Men and women flailing their arms about and bouncing upon the ground to and fro, dancing to the beats. One pocket of gathered crowd were singing what I imagined to be a traditional druidic folk song,

'All round mother earth,
Bring her into birth,
Sweet creatrix of the night and day.
Bring your spirit through,
Rest our thoughts in you,
Guide our feet in the natural way.'

Within the stoned circle itself stood the largest crowd, in prayer to the earth.

Finally, Amy spotted Tom and Susan approaching from the 'Sacred Avenue' and bounded over to them, with arms wide open. She leapt into Tom's arms, who span her round. I made a slow approach and Amy introduced me to the pair, who were kind enough to embrace me with two prolonged and loving hugs.

They each held heavy looking backpacks, that were packed with bottles of cider. 'How's about we crack some of these open out in the fields?' Tom asked.

'Yes, Tomo!' Amy squealed as more and more people gathered at Stonehenge, perhaps thousands by now. Bands were playing, poems were being recited and an ocean of people sat amongst the grass revelling in the ancient celebration of summer solstice.

Tom opened bottles of cider and passed one round to each of us, as the sun slowly lowered and the sky reddened. I felt calm and at peace with the world. 'What took you so long?' Amy asked.

'We woke up late, and then we just took a slow walk,' Susan explained as she took her first sip of cider. We spoke for some time, out amongst the grass and under the constant lowering sun, a slight chill in the air. I explained to Tom and Susan about Uncle Bill, and my planned adventure that Amy had helped liven up; and in turn they told me about their druidic history and practices. They weren't devout druids, but enjoyed the disciplines and they practiced when they could. Not long after we had settled, another group of young adults had sat down a little way from us, and also began drinking from cans of beer.

I noticed one of the guys couldn't take his eyes off Amy. He was ridiculously good looking with dirty blonde dread locks and had the chiseled face of a greek god. Amy caught his glance once or twice, exchanging smiles and waves. A sudden dislike for him came over me, for no reason other than I knew he could easily swipe Amy away.

After getting to know Tom and Susan, and becoming quite tipsy, a sudden loud, thudding horn - or horns - boomed up into the glowing red sky. Everyone got to their feet, including Amy, Tom and Susan and huddled in a huge gathering as the sun began to sink behind the distant tree line. Everyone began to hum in unison with a constant drumming beat booming from the centre. 'May there be peace in the east,' came an elderly man with feathered hat, shouting as loud as he could for all that had gathered. Everyone repeated his words in a united chant, as the sun continued to lower. 'May there be peace in the South. May there be peace in the West. May there be peace in the North, and may there be peace in the world,' he concluded. Suddenly everything went dead silent. The tension and energy electrifying as everyone slowly watched the sun descend with electrifying anticipation. It was here, that I finally felt like I had seen something worth seeing, I felt like part of something. All our faces glowed orange as the bright sun in front of us ever so slowly lowered.

The sun finally vanished from view, and the sky began to turn a dark blue when another thunderous round of horns blew, and the gathered crowd quickly dispersed in joyous song and dance. Now the party was really starting. Waves of people began floating about with their arms raised above their head, jumping from one foot to the other. Many drums beat, flutes and fiddles flailed, and bagpipes bellowed.

I looked over and saw that the man with blonde dread locks had approached Amy and seemingly asked her to dance. She clearly agreed as he quickly led her off into the crowd somewhere. My heart sank, and quickly I felt alone, abandoned. I looked for Tom and Susan, but they were now transfixed in each other's gaze and dancing with their druid fellows. I took a sip of my cider, took one last look at the festival and made my way back to the van.

I sat on the van's side step, swigging away on my cider, listening to the distant beats and chants as the stars slowly began to twinkle through the darkening sky. Some time went by and for whatever reason I didn't have the heart to make my way for Cornwall just yet.

About an hour or so went and I finally felt it was time to leave. I got to my feet and turned to sit myself down in the driver's seat when a familiar voice came from behind. 'I know you're not planning on leaving. The solstice is just getting started and we had a deal.'

I turned to see Amy, Tom, Susan, and regrettably Blondie, the male barbie doll and his friends standing facing me. 'We got some 'shrooms we gonna go ingest in the trees,' he said with a deep, manly and husky voice.

'Oh, no I'm okay. I think I'll probably just hit the road and see if I can get to Cornwall,' was my shaky reply.

He laughed at me and put an arm over Amy's shoulder, 'Whatever dude,' he said as he turned, trying to lead Amy away with him. 'You coming?' he asked her, shocked as she stood rooted to the floor.

'You guys go ahead, I'll stick around and try to get this sack of bore to come join you in a bit,' she said with her sarcastic charisma.

'Don't worry about this guy, he's obviously got things to do,' he persisted, as he tried to force her along with him.

'Get off of me!' demanded Amy, as she finally freed herself.

'Hey!' I yelled, not knowing what had come over me. 'She said she wanted to stay here,' I continued, stepping down from the van.

'Guys,' Susan said, as she tried to step between us. 'Come on. This isn't what solstice is about.'

'Don't you have a dead uncle to see?' he said. At that moment, a fierce rage engulfed my body and all rationale escaped my mind. I advanced on him and I heard Amy plead for this to stop when I felt a sharp thud on my head, before everything silenced and went black.

When I came round, I found myself stirring amongst trees, and under a night sky. The left side of my face throbbed, and my back ached. I found myself laying on an extremely uncomfortable log, my head resting on Amy's thigh. 'Hey,' she said, softly, 'How're you feeling?'

I sat up and rubbed the side of my face. In front of me Tom and Susan were slow dancing, forehead to forehead, and swigging straight vodka from the bottle. 'What happened?' I asked, groggy and dazed.

'That arsehole gave you a good swing, went down like a champ though, defending my honour and all,' she smiled.

'I'm not so sure I quite feel like a champ.'

'Well you're my champ,' she said; but she must have seen something in my eye that she didn't like, because she quickly caught herself, 'Well, a champ for me. At that moment,' she began blushing and growing more and more embarrassed.

There was a short silence between me and Amy, as we watched Tom and Susan. They looked so happy as they danced under the night sky. Sharing the vodka between them, smiling and laughing. Eventually, they embraced each other in a passionate, prolonged kiss. 'They're good together,' I said.

'They're cousins you know?'

'What?!' I said astonished. Amy laughed.

'Yeah.'

'That's weird,' I said, confused.

'Why? They're just happy. Expressing their love for life; their inner joy,' she said, as she took my hand and led me over to them. She placed me in between Tom and Susan as they continued to kiss each other, and she walked round and stood on the other side looking at me. She raised her eyebrows, and smiled. She placed her hand on the back of Susan's head. Susan looked up and seamlessly began kissing Amy. Tom looked up at me and leant in to kiss me.

'No thanks,' I said sternly, trying to sound authoritative despite the fact I had just been knocked out with one punch in front of him a little while before. Tom shrugged at me, and imposed himself onto the girls, igniting a three way kiss. I stood watching awkwardly, feeling uncomfortable. The three of them were so involved that I was able to walk back to the log without them realising. I looked back to Amy a moment, 'Take care,' I said in a soft whisper, as I watched the three glow, carefree.

I smiled to myself and made my way out of the trees. I could see the stones not too far off in the distance, silhouetted in the dark early hours of morning, with various spots of torchlight hitting the rocky surfaces, as lingering revellers continued to celebrate the solstice.

Chapter Four

TRUCKER TALES

I made my way back across the fields feeling a little lost. I was having such fun with Amy, and now I'd probably never see her again. The stars were twinkling fiercely; and as I finally reached the car park I passed the same couple Amy and I had encountered when we parked up earlier this morning.

'Happy solstice, chap,' came the bearded man.

'Happy solstice,' I replied with a gentle smile, as the pair walked off hand in hand together. I threw myself down onto the cushioned driver's seat with a bounce and gently pulled the door closed. I took a deep breath, and exhaled with a longing sigh, resting my forehead on the steering wheel.

'Firecracker that one, in't she?' came Bill's voice suddenly.

'Yeah,' I replied solemnly, without looking up. I could hear random drunken drum beats coming from amongst the stones. I listened intently, closing my eyes. As I let the beats reach me, I pictured Amy and I out amongst the fields that day, just walking and laughing together. 'Jeez!' I said aloud, realising I was really beginning to fall for this girl. I quickly lifted my head up and started the van's engine. I took one last look just incase I might catch a final glimpse of Amy; but she never came. I pulled out of the car park and drove back to the A303.

When I reached the roundabout that would reconnect me to the mighty

'A' road, I was tempted for a moment to turn left and head back towards Amesbury, hoping Amy might return and I could bump into her one more time, this time remembering to take down her number or email address; something that would help me stay in contact with her. At the last minute I came to my senses and veered right, headed west for Cornwall.

I hadn't realised how late - or how early - it had become and my eyes quickly became heavy. My head swayed a little, which was either due to the small amount of cider I had consumed, or because I was concussed. Either way it quickly became obvious that I needed to lay my head down and sleep for a while.

Swiftly I came across a small residential area, that I assumed had been where Susan and Tom stayed the night before. There was a wonderful little inn called The Bell Inn, which appeared to have plenty of stories to tell. Picturesque and situated down the road from Stonehenge? Definitely had stories to tell. It sat deadly silent in the early hours, without a stirring amongst its windows; it felt almost as if it was there to peacefully welcome me into town.

A small parking lay-by was free a little further along, but I didn't feel comfortable with the thought of staying there the night. Maybe it was out of worry that I would be in someone's designated driveway, or I was just being a plain coward looking for excuses. I drove on, figuring that there would be another lay-by soon enough, that wasn't surrounded by houses.

As I passed out of the small town, the road became shrouded in complete darkness. The disappearance of street lamps became evident and my journey suddenly became more ominous. Everything was pitch black, bar the little light that the old camper struggled to provide, 'Careful now,' came Bill.

The next rest point didn't seem to be on its way, and my eyes were getting heavier and heavier. I rolled down the windows to let the cool night air smack my face and I found my mind wander gently back to

Amy. What was she up to now? Had she found somewhere to stay? Was she still dancing away amongst the trees? How was she going to get back home? I smiled again, as I saw her swirling in the rain back in Amesbury the morning before.

'Watch it!' Bill suddenly screamed. I quickly snapped back to reality, after slipping into auto-pilot and saw a small animal racing out into the road in front of me. I gripped the wheel tightly and swerved fiercely out of the way, narrowly missing the small furred creature. I felt a nasty thud beneath me and I was launched into the air a few inches before crashing back into my seat.

The van had hit the kerb. I managed to swerve back into the lane, before smacking my foot down on the brake; screeching to a halt. Taking a deep breath, I stared out into nothingness; the animal probably long gone and completely oblivious to how close it had come to death. My heart pounded against my chest, and I found it hard to catch my breath. 'That's enough excitement for one day I think,' came Bill, as he looked up at me with an unimpressed gaze. He had spilled his Jack Daniel's down his top, and began cursing under his breath, trying to dab it dry with a tissue.

'Agreed.' I rubbed my eyes, and slapped the sides of my face repeatedly before deciding to press on as quickly as possible, in search of somewhere I could rest my eyes.

Eventually I approached a lay-by and could see that a cargo lorry had already parked up, though thankfully there was still room for my camper to slip in and park up behind it.

As I approached I could see a small glow from the truck driver's cigarette tip, as he stood outside in the dark, on one leg, leaning the other foot against the large front tyre. I yanked up on the handbrake and sat quietly looking at the driver, a little nervous. He didn't budge; instead he just took the last drag of his smoke before flicking it out onto the road.

I decided I was safe enough and jumped down out of the van,

slowly walking round to the other side to inspect my own tyre and the van's skirting; just in case there were damages from hitting the kerb. It was dark and I had to quickly open the passenger's door and reach over to pick up my phone from the dashboard, before switching on the torch it had built into it.

I started inspecting thoroughly, and thankfully everything seemed as good as could be. 'Everything alright?' I heard the faint voice come from behind me. I jumped a little, as I was already anxious about sharing the lay-by with the man.

'Yes thank you,' I replied shakily, continuing with my thorough search. The driver had walked over by this point and stood behind me. His grubby work trousers and heavy boots were in my peripheral.

'What you lookin' for?' he asked, in a northern accent.

'Hopefully nothing. I hit the kerb a little bit down the road, and I just want to make sure it hadn't caused any damage.'

'Right,' he said as he knelt down, inspecting the van himself. 'Well for starters this tyre's gotta go!'

'What?'

'Look at this bubble 'ere. You can't be driving on that,' he explained as he grabbed my hand tightly and shone the torch onto it. A small air bubble had popped up that I completely missed.

'What does that mean?'

'It means you can't be driving. Not long distance anyway. Where you off to?' he asked, rubbing the tips of his fingers over the protrusion, making further inspections.

'Cornwall.'

'Cornwall! It'll have to come off before you head down there, pal.'

'Oh,' I said. I stood up, rooted to the spot, not knowing what to say or do. I wasn't a car kind of guy, and didn't have the faintest idea how to change a tyre. By this point the driver had also got to his feet and began walking back to his lorry. 'Uh, excuse me,' I called out. I saw him swivel around and face me once more. 'I'm sorry to bother you but, how do I change a tyre? And where do I get a new one?'

I heard the driver chuckle under his breath, before his heavy boots thudded the ground as he slowly walked back over to me. He reached into his back pocket and pulled out a rather crumpled cigarette box and lit another smoke. His face glowed orange for a brief minute from the flame of his lighter, which he flicked shut and shoved back into his pocket. He took a deep drag before blowing smoke in my face, not in an aggressive manner mind you.

'You not got a spare?' he asked.

I looked at him blankly. 'Uhm, maybe. I've only just got the van, you see.'

He sighed and took another drag of his cigarette. 'Well, it's clearly not on the front. I take it it's a water cooled model?' he asked. Again I could do nothing but shrug my shoulders. The lorry driver walked round the back and peered through the rear window. 'Here you go.'

I walked round and peered through. Embarrassingly there was a tyre laid down with a load of tools beside it, in a well behind the back seating and bed that I hadn't even realised existed. 'Good to see you got yourself a jack. That's a start. Pop 'er open and we'll get you sorted.'

I obliged and lifted the boot open, yanking out the spare tyre and carrying it round to the front, whilst the driver pulled out a few tools and dropped them down by the side of the van. 'I'm Alex,' I said, still not the best at dealing with awkward social situations.

'Dan. See you like your booze.'

'Excuse me?' I replied confused.

'The blanket got caught on the tools as I lifted them out. Don't worry I'm not one to judge. I enjoy a rum myself,' he said, throwing the jack under the van and lifting it off the ground. I stood a moment, trying not to look too flummoxed; eventually I returned back to the boot of the van and was pleasantly surprised by what I found.

There was a large, bulky cardboard box filled with different litre bottles of alcohol. Mostly Jack Daniel's, but there was also Smirnoff vodka and Captain Morgan's Rum. I laughed inside, admiring Uncle Bill's alcohol stash before walking back round to the side of the van.

Dan got to work changing my tyre diligently whilst I helped where I could. I felt a fool watching this man get down and do the labours of my grief, whilst I stood awkwardly, emasculated. 'So, driving a lorry must be fun?' I asked, attempting small talk in order to fill the silence.

'Oh pal, you wouldn't believe,' he replied as he continued to slug away.

'Nice looking truck. Bit intimidating to drive I'd imagine?'

'No, no! Feels good.'

Dan went on to tell me stories about his life on the road. He was a family man, and had a small boy with his wife. He spoke lovingly about them, and smiled fondly.

Dan slowly lowered the van back onto the ground, and wiped his hands on his trousers. 'Right, that'll do you. Make sure you get rid of this when you reach Cornwall. It's no good to anyone now, bud.'

'Thank you,' I smiled as I rolled the bubbled tire round to the back, throwing it into the boot. 'Goodnight,' I said as I came back and stepped up into the side.

'Oh I wish. You caught me at a good time; lucky really as I was just waking up and getting ready to set out again. Sleep well lad, and get to Cornwall safe,' Dan said as he lit yet another smoke and made his way for the lorry.

I watched him a moment before calling out after him, 'Would you like a bottle of rum for the trouble?'

'How could I say no to that?' he replied. I smiled and raced round to the boot, yanking out a bottle of Morgan's before handing it to him. 'Ta,' he said before returning to his lorry.

I climbed up into the van and closed all the curtains before pulling out the bed. I undressed and finally threw myself down. For a moment I looked up at the roof and saw Amy. Her strawberry scent was still over the sheets and my mind was cast back to our night together.

I heard Dan's engine roar up and his wheels roll over the tarmac before he gradually disappeared down the A303. I thought of everything I had experienced since leaving home. I was spending my first night alone in Bill's camper, in completely new and strange surroundings. A sense of independence surged within and an excited fearless audacity came about me. I flung off my underwear and dived under the quilts naked as the day I was born. Was this what freedom felt like? I closed my eyes and gently drifted off into deep sleep, a lasting smile across my face.

Chapter Five

BATH AND WEST SHOW

The song of birds chirping from the trees beside me, and the increasingly more frequent roar of cars began to rile me from my sleep. The van had become very hot and I awoke gasping for air. I had foolishly kept the windows shut throughout the night, and now I was beginning to bake in my own oven.

I leapt up out of bed and yanked open the side door, desperate to get oxygen into my lungs. The moment the door locked open, I jumped out and my bare feet landed harshly on small stones and bits of gravel.

'Oh my lord!' yelled a woman of about forty, horrified. I then realised I had valiantly decided to sleep naked last night; and I was no longer alone in the lay-by.

'Sorry,' I whined, with my tail between my legs - so to speak. Quickly covering my bits I jumped back into the van, as the poor woman's husband wrapped his arm round her and lead her back to their car, with a chuckle to himself. I threw the door shut, and quickly fumbled through my backpack for fresh underwear and a clean pair of jeans.

My bag wasn't packed very well, and this was the first chance I had to go through it. I only now noticed that the van had a very tiny wardrobe built into it. I quickly put away the bed before throwing my bag down onto the sofa with the intention of putting the little amount of clothing I had into the wardrobe.

As I pulled out my few tops and a third pair of jeans, I opened the door to the wardrobe and was met by something completely out of place. Three drink optics had been screwed into the back of the wardrobe.

An almost empty bottle of Jack Daniel's, half a bottle of vodka, and practically a full bottle of Captain Morgan's. 'Finish off the Jack for me,' came Bill from behind. I turned round surprised and wide eyed. 'What?' he asked.

'It was bad enough that I was seeing you in the mirror, now I'm seeing you in person? It's a little worrying.'

'It's all in your head, son.'

'Exactly!' I countered, worried I might be going insane. Uncle Bill took a swig of his tumbler, and I began shoving my clothes back in my bag; clearly there'd be no room for them in the tiny space left by the optics.

When I looked up, Bill had gone. I saw in my peripheral the bottles hanging in the wardrobe. 'Screw it, one won't hurt.' I reached for a mug, and threw it under the Jack Daniel's optic before taking a swift, clean swig.

I threw on a top and shoes and opened the side door once more. Thankfully the other car had moved on by now and I was saved from the embarrassment of having to face them again. I sat on the side step, as Bill often did, and sipped from a mug of black coffee. I felt the sun's rays beat down on my scalp, as I soaked up some vitamin D. I was faced with bushes and trees. I could still hear the birds singing to one another, and the sky was perfectly blue and clear.

As I came to the end of my coffee, and mentally prepared myself for another day on the road, I saw a large goose glide gracefully through the sky above. He was alone, and something about him was very majestic. I wondered where he was heading, and whether he himself knew. Was he flying towards his flock, or away from it? I toasted my mug to it, before it vanished from view. I finished my coffee and climbed into the driver's seat, starting the engine and getting back onto the A303.

The sun was shining in its full glory, and I rolled down the window. My elbow rested on the frame, as the sun's heat warmed my forearm. Peter Green's CD was still in the player, and his song 'Albatross' started up; my mind cast back to Amy once more. I looked over to the passenger seat and wished that she was still there; then I remembered back to yesterday morning when she tried taking off her top. 'You worry too much,' I recounted her say. I smiled at the memory, and with great awkward difficulty began to lift my own top off over my head.

After great effort, and almost running myself off the road for a third time, I was able to feel the sun blaze down onto my bare chest, the cooling air breezing onto me from the open window.

It was only a few hundred yards when I had already hit a brown road sign! 'Longleat.' I felt my anxiety begin to stir in me. My heart was beginning to beat faster, and I questioned myself. 'Do I turn off or don't I?'

The turning was fast approaching and I couldn't decide. I checked in my rear view mirror to see if I would inconvenience anyone by slowing down. There was a sporty looking Ford Focus whizzing up behind me and without realising my foot lowered ever so slightly onto the accelerator; and I drove straight past the turning for Longleat.

'Oi you! That's not what we agreed! You'll regret that one, mate. Right nice place, Longleat. Beautiful,' cried Bill, completely unimpressed. I ignored him and looked back to the Focus, which had now practically hit my rear bumper, before it sped past, overtaking me at a ridiculous speed. 'Better turn off at the next one,' he warned. I looked back at him, and he was staring me dead in the eye.

I drove along, bobbing my head to the beat of Peter Green, feeling cool and free. It was some time before I hit another brown sign; and when I saw it my stomach sank, and my heart started up again. I turned the music up and once again drove straight passed 'Stour Head Garden and House.'

'Sorry,' I said, looking back to Uncle Bill. This time he didn't even look my way. His brow furrowed, and he looked out the window next to him, taking another sip of his Jack Daniels. I realised I had messed up, and let us both down. I was here for an adventure, and so far all I had done was coward out of things. I nodded and convinced myself the next sign that came, would be our destination for the day.

Once again I drove down for quite a stretch, the whole time Bill looking out the window like a sulking boy. I smiled, 'Cheer up,' to which he replied with a curse under his breath; which could have been mistaken for 'Duck cough.'

There was a sense of banter in his tone of course, but also a hint of seriousness. He was quiet for the rest of the way, and I knew the sooner I hit a brown sign the better. I now anxiously anticipated one, rather than dread the thing. Eventually it came, and I perked up in excitement, 'Here we are,' I called back, flicking on my indicator to come off; and squinting my eyes trying to make out the writing on the sign. 'Wincanton Racecourse,' I read aloud.

I felt my stomach drop, and my excitement swiftly evaporate, I had to visit a racecourse?! One which I didn't even know to be open or not; but I made a promise that I would come off and visit, so that's what I was going to do. I slowly veered off, about to exit when I heard the rescuing voice from behind, 'Oh bugger that! You don't need to go to a bloody racecourse. Make sure you come off the next one though!'

I smiled, relieved and quickly pulled us back onto the A road, as cars behind beeped and hooted before overtaking swiftly. Another long stretch of road laid before us, but now both Bill and I were anticipating our next adventure, when finally, 'Bath and West Show. Perfect,' yelled Bill. I pulled us off and followed the signs, having never heard of it.

When we finally arrived, we were ushered into the specified parking area, which was free - a relief after the extortion I had suffered at Stonehenge - and I found myself staring out of the windscreen, daunted at the thought of attending what was some kind of festival. In front of me I could see a spiralling slide tower, with screaming kids whizzing round one after the other. In the distance I could hear a live country rock band playing somewhere. The car park was full and people were passing through consistently.

'This is more like it,' came Bill. I let out a laugh and pulled the keys out of the ignition. I took a deep breath, and moved into the back of the van, before swinging open the wardrobe and pouring myself another shot of J. D. Knocking it back, I coughed a little and made my way out of the van. 'Have fun,' Bill called out after me.

The first thing I noticed as I made my way across the grassed car park and into the show itself, was the sheer joy on everyone's face. There was a lot of families, and plenty of young adults like myself. What first met me was some sort of fair ground. Along with the slide tower, there were food stalls, and beer stalls. There was even a petting zoo. I also stumbled across a small stage, which is where the music had been coming from. The band consisted of a drummer, bassist, acoustic guitarist and singer. The instrumentalists were all young men, and the singer was a young blonde girl wearing a straw cowboy hat, denim shorts and a red chequered top. I smiled.

I spent a long time just walking through the field, wondering what there was for me to do. I decided my first act would be buying a beer. There was a whole row of trailer bars, and food stands next to the stage, and the organisers had laid out sun loungers scattered in front of both. Some were facing the musicians, and some were facing away. I stood for a little while, watching the band and nodding my head, before plonking myself down in a lounger to watch the people go by and soak up the atmosphere.

There were kids running around chasing each other, playing. There were groups of young adults about my age, with drinks in hand and laughing, and there were young couples hand in hand. I sat for a good hour, just listening to the music and watching all the people enjoy their day.

After a while, and two or three beers later I decided to take a walk and see what else this place had to offer. Whether it was the beer or the infectious atmosphere I felt happy, with a light feeling inside. This was definitely worth leaving my dark and gloomy room for.

I went out of my way to walk through the petting zoo, which boasted an array of animals; including goats, sheep, piglets and ducks all with the same excited attitude as us humans. There was a grand horse show, with intimidatingly giant Shire Horses, that towered over everyone. Strong and proud, parading round and pulling carts and buggies.

Inside a metal barn, I found a whole host of cattle and sheep. I assumed they were being sold to farmers who had travelled from across the country to attend this show.

After spending some time looking at all the well-groomed cattle and sheep, I realised I had finished my beer, and I was having too good a time to not have another one. As I stepped out from the impressively large barn, I heard a commotion come from down one of the side walkways.

'But da'!' whinged a young boy.

'I'm sorry son,' the man replied in a sorrowful voice, with a thick Devonshire accent. 'Yer know I gotsta attend certain things when they call. We'll get them next time, o'right?' he concluded, ruffling the small boy's hair.

The young lad looked up at his father with teary eyes, as he grasped onto a small pony's reigns that stood beside him. 'But we've been practicing all year,' he wept.

I stood for a moment, as my curiosity got the better of me. The farmer bent down to his son's level and said something more to him, before embracing his inconsolable boy.

I don't know why, but something inside urged me forward, and before I could stop myself I was standing next to them. 'Is everything okay?' I asked.

'Oh yeah, just... well my boy was excited to take part in the horse race yer see, but I'm afraid we got to be going. Duty calls,' he started, and then looked down to his son.

'I can stay without you. I can look after myself,' the boy pleaded.

'Now, now Toby, I've told you yer not old enough for that yet.' I saw the deep hurt in the young boy's eyes, and I could relate. Many times I've been in similar situations and felt let down.

'Well how long will you be? I can look after him; I'll make sure he gets to the race,' I offered quickly, again without realising I had done so until it was too late. Toby leapt with excitement.

'Yeah, yeah, yeah! Please!' I looked at Toby's father, and could see the inner conflict. It was a little amusing, but I understood that he wouldn't want to leave his boy with a complete stranger. There was a brief silence whilst he pondered.

'Tell you what, I'll walk with yers to the signing in desk and get ya set up, then this kind chap can chaperone yous until I get back. O'right?' The boy's tears transformed into a beaming smile and he tended to his pony and prepared to set off for the race. His father turned to me, and with a deadly intimidating stare he enforced, 'I'll be letting the people know that yer just a chaperone and in no way are yer to leave the pen with my boy. Understand?'

I nodded and smiled. 'Of course.' We made for the signing in desk, when I wondered what the heck I had got myself in to.

The signing in process was quick and easy, and as Toby's father stated he made the stewards aware of our situation, before wishing his son luck and disappearing into the crowd. Toby's excitement quickly vanished when he realised his father really wasn't going to stay. He looked sad again and he led his pony into a designated area; quickly beginning to brush his pony. 'What's wrong?' I asked.

'My dad an' I been practising for this a whole year.'

'That's great! You don't have anything to worry about then; puts you in with a good chance of winning.'

'But he's not here to see it. It was something we were supposed to be doing together.' I stood stunned a moment. What was I supposed to say to console this boy?

'Look, sometimes our dads can't be here to see the things that we desperately want them to. At your age, we take it personally but trust me, when you get older and have responsibilities of your own you'll understand,' I said, completely unsure what I was doing. Toby nodded and continued to groom the horse, with the faintest of forced smiles.

Some minutes went by and Toby made final checks with his pony, and saddle. I looked around the field that had various young boys and girls that would be competing against Toby, and I felt a strange competitive streak stir inside. I wanted to give Toby some encouraging words of advice, but as I didn't know the first thing about horse racing, I decided to just watch on.

Finally they called all racers to the field, and I left Toby with a friendly pat on the back and wished him luck, before heading to the spectating area.

There were hoops elevated on poles, and at various checkpoints, objects had been laid onto the ground. All the horses and their riders lined up alongside one another and there was a crisp tension in the air. Everything went dead silent, 'Come on Toby!' I suddenly found myself screaming, out of pure excitement. He looked over at me and gave me an embarrassed smile, looking around him.

'Get set. Go!' and a pistol let out. In the blink of an eye all the young ponies swept over the ground like bullets and made their way to the first pole. As Toby reached his first check point I found myself biting my lip and my eyes squinting, as his small body slowly lowered from the horse and got dangerously close to the floor. 'Come on,' I said to myself quietly, as Toby picked up a small item from the floor in one swift movement, turned, and raced back to the small bucket that had been at his feet at the start of the race.

Things were close, and Toby sat in fourth place. As the young girl in the lead threw her first object into her bucket, and raced back to the second check point, I realised it was a race to see who could get all the scattered items into their bucket first.

'Go Toby, go!' I screamed at the top of my voice.

It wasn't long until Toby found himself in third place with just two more items to go, and I couldn't help myself but jump up and down, tapping my hand repeatedly on the metal barriers that had been put out to keep spectators safe from the onslaught of fiercely focussed horses. The young lad in second place accidentally let his item slip, and he had to turn back to retrieve it; which placed Toby second!

Toby quickly found himself inches off the girl in first place, and they both placed their items back in their bucket, before racing off again with immediate haste. 'You got this Toby!' I kept shouting, as my voice started to become hoarse.

As Toby and the young girl made their way for the final object, they were made to pick up what looked like a small plastic joust. They yanked them up from the ground ferociously and continued at nail biting speed. Just then I felt a stern pat on the back, and I looked behind me to see Toby's father standing beside me. I looked at him curiously, before he stated, 'Werk can wait,' in his thick country accent. 'Let's go Toby!'

Somehow Toby must have heard his father's voice yell over everyone else's as he looked over, smiled and focused himself on the race once more. Suddenly Toby was going faster, and he was neck and neck with the young girl. They both threw their jousts into a ringed hoop, turned and raced back.

Sadly Toby was a little slow in turning, and he fell behind. I could see the frustration in the poor little lad's face, as he fell behind more and more. I could feel his father's energy sink too and I looked to him. He didn't look away from the race, and although Toby's victory was looking less and less likely, he still had hope. 'Come on Toby, we've werked on this,' he said under his breath.

I looked back to the race, and saw that Toby gradually lowered his body and to my surprise he was catching up again! To my astonishment

Toby made a comeback, and the leading pair had left the rest of the racers far behind. They were neck and neck once more and only a few yards away from the finish line!

'Yes!' me and Toby's father screamed as he stretched in front by just a few inches. They were almost upon their individual boxes and they lowered their jousts as they both prepared to drop the hoops into the boxes. Toby had the lead and was seconds away from winning the race after an amazing comeback.

Then there was a deep sigh from the crowd in unison. 'No!' his father screamed, startling me. Toby tried to drop his hoop into the box but hit the edge. It bounced away, as the young girl successfully dropped her hoop into her own box seconds later. She had won the race. Toby, not giving up respectably turned, hooked up the hoop and threw it down into his box just in time to be placed second.

Once the other racers had completed the task, the crowd gradually dispersed, not hanging around for the small medal ceremony. Toby's father had glumly returned to Toby's side; and I could see them off in the distance talking to each other, before Toby's dad embraced him in a consoling hug. I smiled and decided that I had had enough excitement for one day.

I quickly returned to the van, threw in the keys and got back to the A303. Toby's fighting spirit had left it's mark on me, and I drove for a little while with a great feeling of pride. With all the excitement, and standing in the glaring sun all day, I found my eyes getting heavy. It was five in the evening by this point and the sunset was gorgeous; and so with the new found pride and feeling of excitement, I decided to be a little more adventurous, and park up for another night in a lay-by. I felt great, and no longer had the need to rush down to Cornwall. Now I was going to savour every minute of it. 'See,' came Bill, 'being spontaneous feels good.'

I smiled and agreed, and then pulled over into the next lay-by I came to. I left the battery running and played a Stones album. I reached down into my backpack and for the first time pulled out a book. I slung off my shoes, threw out the bed, slid the side door open and read until it was too dark to do so. I was stuffed from eating numerous cheese burgers throughout the day- and naughtily a bit more than tipsy from all the beer.

Once the sun had completely set, the bird's singing was replaced by the melodic hooting of owls out amongst the trees. I closed my book, and my door; and I fell into a deep calming sleep almost immediately.

That didn't last long however. I was shaken awake by the startling sound of a screeching car that came to a sudden halt behind me in the lay-by and I leapt up with fright. I could hear yelling and what sounded to me like a tussle; then as I gently pulled back a bit of my rear curtain, I saw a man that seemed to have been beaten very badly, with a bloodied face thrown out of the car, before it screeched off again.

I waited a moment, frozen with fear, until the man's agonising groans became unbearable and I quickly threw on some clothes and ran outside.

'Are you okay?' I called out. He had blood all over his face, with scratches, grazes and cuts. He had a small greying beard and clean shaven head, completely bald. The man didn't reply, instead he continued to grimace around on the floor. 'Hello, are you okay?' I repeated.

Eventually I decided to go over and tend to the man myself. I got him off the ground before leading him over to the van; sitting him down on the side step. 'Just sit tight,' I stated as reassuringly as I could, before pulling out a mug and getting him a shot of vodka from the optics. My hands were shaking. 'I'll call the police and they'll get those guys in no time,' I said, making my way into the front passenger's seat as I kept my phone in the glove compartment.

'No,' he said. 'No, don't do that.'

Chapter Six

INTO THE TREES

I fetched the man another shot of vodka, and made myself a whiskey before joining him on the side of the bed. It was awkward, and I suddenly realised I had put myself in a potentially dangerous situation. 'How are you feeling,' I asked, desperate to break the silence.

'I'll mend.'

'Are you sure you don't want me to call you an ambulance? Police?'

'No,' he snapped. Another awkward silence filled the air as the man winced. He was clearly mixed up with some dangerous people and I knew I had to find a way of getting this man out of the van and drive away as swiftly as I could. I became fidgety and continued to make us both alcoholic drinks, as I tried desperately to come up with a plan.

I got up as our mugs emptied once more, and walked over to my optics. I was on my last Jack Daniels before I would have to change the bottle, and the man had made a significant dent in the vodka too. The van swirled and I realised that on top of all the whiskeys I had nervously poured myself, I had had a lot to drink at the Bath and West show too.

'How 'bout I get you a cab,' I asked, slurring my words. There was no response, and an uncomfortably long silence. Confused, I turned to find that he was suddenly standing over me, uncomfortably close and staring at me intently. A sudden sense of despair hit me; then everything went black.

I awoke with a thumping headache, and surrounded by bushes, with twigs poking at me all over. The alcohol hadn't worn off and I was dazed. I sat up awkwardly and pushed myself out of the bushes. That's when the sickening feeling struck. I looked out to the lay-by and the van had gone. I swayed and almost collapsed. I cursed at the top of my voice and ran back into the gravelled resting point. I looked every which way to try and find the van but it was no use; it was gone. 'No, no, no, no,' I continued to repeat, lifting my hands up to my head in despair.

Everything just sank, all the excitement I had felt a few hours ago as I watched Toby in his race, now seemed like a whole world away. I reached into my back pocket to pull out my phone and immediately call the police, when I realised my phone was in the van's glove compartment. I let out more curses.

My eyes welled and a few tears slid down my face. Probably the most cherished thing Bill had left me and now it was gone. He loved that van so much, and I had grown to feel the same way. It had strangely become a part of me; a friend.

I had no idea what I was going to do, or how I was going to get home; or to Par even! It was pitch black and the middle of the night, and the A303 was dead. Surely there would be a truck soon and I could flag them into the lay-by and explain to them what had happened.

I sat and waited. What seemed like hours had only been thirty minutes, and I grew more and more scared and upset. I began to shiver as I only had a t-shirt on. Never had I wanted to see Bill in my mind more than I did right now; to guide me, lecture me, anything, but he would not come.

Tears ran down my cheek freely and I wished I had never left home. I should have stayed in my room until the funeral and driven down with mum. What was going to happen to me? What if another car didn't arrive for hours?

I got to my feet and decided I would climb back through the trees and into the field behind me, to see if there were any buildings close by that I could walk to and get help.

The field was dark, and I could hardly see in front of me. I could just about glimpse a group of silhouetted trees, huddled together in a cluster, and beyond those flickered some lights. It was apparent it would take me a while to get to them, and that I may be better off staying in the lay-by; but I set out across the field, desperate to be anywhere but here.

As I found myself making progress into the field, thudding beats from a car's radio echoed into the air behind me, laughter and revelling. I heard their tyres screech as they whizzed round the corner and off into the distance again. I kicked the ground and cursed, no time to run back and grab their attention. I continued towards the distant specks of light.

I wrapped my arms around myself, rubbing them, desperately trying to keep warm. The ground was uneven and I repeatedly lost balance. The sound of owls hooting did little to relax me now, and I just felt sick. I've never been so helpless and vulnerable my whole life, and all because I had decided to go on a bloody adventure. If you can even call it that!

Eventually I reached the small group of trees, and decided that I would cut through them, rather than round them. The trees were daunting at first, but I quickly found comfort amongst them; as if they were cradling me in my deep sorrowful regret.

The sounds of crickets helped, though I was still pretty shaken. So much so that when a bird flapped its wings, snapping twigs with it, I let out a less than manly yell. 'Oi!' came a voice; and again I jumped.

When I looked over I saw Uncle Bill, sitting in a fold out fishing chair, and smoking a cigarette. 'Uncle Bill?'

'Come over 'ere,' he said, and I did so. This whole day had been a complete whirlwind, and I started to wonder whether I was concussed. 'What on earth are you cryin' for?'

I didn't reply immediately, knowing that I couldn't possibly be seeing him sitting in a bloody fishing chair, smoking a cigarette in the middle of the night, amongst a bunch of trees. Eventually, however, I decided to play ball. 'I've lost your van.'

'So?'

Stunned, I looked at him for another moment. 'It's gone. You trusted me with your most treasured possession, and I lost it.'

'First of all, it was stolen from you,' he said sternly. 'After doing a very noble thing. You're heart was in the right place, and nobody could ever be mad at you for that. Secondly, it's just a bleedin' van. Be thankful you still have your life.'

I was so overwhelmed by this point that I didn't have anything to say. 'I've been stabbed, beaten up so many times I've broken just about every bone in my body. Even died for four minutes. Don't worry. It's just a van. Shit happens and we move on. That's life.'

He pushed himself up awkwardly from his low chair and walked over to me with a grin on his face. 'We gotta toughen you up son. Here, have a drink of this and pull yourself together,' he said, handing me his tumbler. I wiped and closed my eyes before taking a deep breath. I took a gulp of his whiskey and when I opened my eyes again, he was gone; and I was alone in the trees once more.

I looked around as the wind blew gently, when I realised I could hear the faint wailing of sirens. It had to be something to do with my van! I pegged it back towards the lay-by as fast as I could. I got close and I saw blue lights illuminating the trees back on the A303.

Just as I made it back to the trees, and began climbing through, two police cars whizzed past and whipped round the bend. I forced my way through, cutting and scraping my face as I went, and continued to leg it down the road. I wouldn't stop until I had recovered my van. It was a longer run than I had anticipated, and I could hardly breath when I finally saw the return of flashing blue lights amongst the trees. I screamed in determination and found the energy to sprint just that little bit further.

When I finally reached the commotion, there were two police cars on either side of the van, which had veered off the road and into a slight dip. The driver's door was open and a police dog was let off its lead, and it went leaping into the field, sniffing.

'That's-my-van,' I managed, trying desperately to catch my breath.

'Calm down,' the police officer told me authoritatively and sticking out one hand as he took a cautious step back. 'Breathe.'

'That's- my van,' I repeated slowly, finding my breath. 'It was stolen from me down the road as I tried to help the man that stole it,' I explained. I went on to tell him the whole story about how the man had been kicked from a car, and after I had taken him to my van he had attacked me and stole the van.

'Do you have any proof the van is yours?'

I was silent. 'Uh- no,' I said shocked. I had no way of proving this van was mine, and I wasn't even sure whether it was in my name. Then something else hit me, I didn't know whether I was insured for the vehicle or not!

'I can call my mum and have her explain to you. My phone should be inside,' I said, now extremely nervous and wondering if I had just walked myself into getting arrested. The police officer instructed me to stay where I was, as they would need to search the van for more evidence, as the man they suspect to have been driving was possibly an armed and wanted criminal.

The officer said other things but I wasn't listening any more. The image of the man sitting in my van came back to me, and I realised just how true Bill's words were, about being lucky to have my life. I felt a swirling in my stomach, and my head went light; before I knew it I bent over and spewed to the side of the road.

By now the officer had grown very suspicious of me and began questioning me. He quickly realised how drunk I was, and my nervous anxiety only made things worse. I told him everything and in the end we agreed that, as I was well over the limit anyway, I would go down to the station with him and have everything straightened out. The van would be towed back to the station and if everything worked out, I would be free to leave with the van as soon as I had slept the intoxication off.

Chapter Seven

A NIGHT IN NICK

I woke up in the most uncomfortable position. I took a moment to get my surroundings before sitting up. I was perched on a small metal bench, in the reception area of the police station.

I had on a really old and grubby black jumper, that had been given to me by a kind officer from their lock up, to stop me shivering through the night. At first I was apprehensive to put it on, as I didn't particularly want to be wearing the jumper of a murderer, or worse their victim. After a while though I couldn't take the shivering any longer and threw it on before putting my head down for some time.

'Morning,' called the police officer from behind a windowed reception. 'I'll just call the Sergeant down, and she can explain to you what's happening.' I smiled and nodded gently, still trying to wake myself up.

There were a couple of other people in the reception area, that had obviously been watching me as I slept, and we both embarrassingly avoided eye contact. 'Morning Alex,' came a delicate voice. I looked over and a striking Police Sergeant came out from a very heavy door, walking over to me.

'Morning,' I replied. She came and sat down next to me before patting a folder on her lap. 'Wow. You're attractive,' I said, still a little dazed from my sleep deprived state.

She gave me a quizzical smile, 'That's not very appropriate now is it.'

'Oh, no I'm sorry. I'm not trying to hit on you or anything. But you are beautiful; I just mean that most police ladies aren't usually attractive-'

'-So,' she quickly interrupted, thankfully, 'You and your van are free to go. We've spoken with your mother Alex and she has confirmed everything with us. We've also checked our database and we see that everything is in order.'

I sat a minute. 'Thank you,' I said, getting to my feet. The police lady stood too and asked me to sign a couple of forms, gave me back my phone, and handed me the keys to the van, whilst it was brought into the car park out front by another officer.

I walked out of the station and into the car park. Immediately I noticed the dents in the bumper and frame work. I couldn't be bothered to even think about how I was going to get them fixed. All I knew was I just wanted to get down to Cornwall as soon as possible now, where I knew I was safe, and could relax.

Firstly, I had to call Mum and find out how it all worked out so well. I climbed up into the van, and pulled out my phone. She went on to explain to me that her and Uncle Bill had actually placed me as a named driver on the van's insurance over a year ago in anticipation.

All of a sudden, I became terribly home sick. Hearing Mum's voice for the first time since I set out struck a nerve in me. Of course she had been terribly worried after receiving a call from the police and desperately wanted to hear my voice. I snapped inside and told her I was coming home.

She wouldn't have any of it, even after I reminded her that I had shared the van with an armed criminal hours before. She wanted me to continue my journey to Cornwall, even if I had to do what I originally planned, and just drive straight there now; so that's what I set out to do.

Chapter Eight

CASTLE IN THE PARK

I raced out of the police station car park, after setting my phone's GPS for the A303 - though I was very tempted to have it direct me to Cornwall via the quickest route, even if that did mean I wouldn't see the A303 again; but I decided against it at the last minute. I still had to honour Uncle Bill.

The road no longer excited me anymore, and I found my mind wandered very little; and when it did, it quickly snapped back to concentrating on driving safely, and as swift as the van would take me.

Everything about the journey had become stiff now, and I didn't get any enjoyment out of it; Uncle Bill hadn't made an appearance either.

The road dragged on, and the rolling, rich green hills of the English countryside no longer made an impact. The novelty had well and truly worn off.

Some time went by and I eventually found myself back on the A303. It wasn't far up the road from the incident, and I recognised one or two pieces of scenery from the night before, as I sat in the back of a police car, being escorted to the station.

I approached a roundabout and felt my stomach begin to rumble. I then realised that I hadn't, you know, been to the toilet in that way, since I left home.

'Gonna have to use the bucket, mate,' came Bill suddenly. I looked back, unimpressed.

'I'm not doing a number two in a bucket.'

Bill let out hoarse laugh, very much amused. 'You got no choice. That's camper life. It's all part of the adventure!'

'I'll just find a toilet,' I replied. Thankfully I came to a roundabout very quickly. The sign explained that the A303 would continue on to Minster Industrial Area, and I hoped there would be services coming up.

Although there were no services, when I approached the roundabout I could see a petrol garage just off the exit before the one I'd take to continue on the A road.

'That'll do,' I said, approaching the roundabout and indicating. Ironically, as I was coming off there was a brown roadside, indicating that 'Barrington Court' was close by.

'Oooh,' came Uncle Bill.

'Don't even think about it,' I interrupted sharply.

'Hey, watch your tone,' he warned. My stomach sank a little, as I briefly lost myself, and I pulled into the petrol station. I jumped out of the van, closing the door harshly and raced inside.

I asked the man behind the counter where the toilets were and he pointed them out, tucked away in the back. When I got in there I was met by a most gag inducing smell. The strongest scent of shit and piss I had ever come across. My throat tightened and I retched. Flies buzzed, and in every corner spiders' webs were filled with the trapped winged insects. There were bundles of toilet paper all over the floor, and the bin was filled with empty beer cans.

I took a deep breath and lined the toilet seat with paper, before I plonked myself down and did my business; holding my breath for as long as I could.

Finishing as quickly as possible, I spent a considerable amount of effort washing my hands, until I was sure I had washed off whatever germs I might have picked up in this cesspit. I picked up as much toilet towel as I could, wrapped them round the door handle, and raced out of there as quick as my legs could take me, retching along the way.

I leapt into the van and whizzed back onto the A303. 'How was it?' asked Uncle Bill, almost as if he already knew.

'I think I would have preferred the bucket.'

Bill let out another mighty laugh and took a sip of Jack Daniels. 'Yep, that sounds about right. Camper lesson one, avoid roadside toilets at all costs. Anyway, buckets aren't that bad; quite freeing really. The breeze is nice.'

I rolled my eyes and continued driving. 'Next stop, Par,' I said, determinedly.

I drove silently for a long time, ignoring any brown sign that cropped up. I passed Illminster, and then Horton without so much of a whisper from Bill. I suddenly found myself welcomed by the rich rolling hills of the English countryside again. I tried not to bat an eyelid, and pay no attention; but deep down I was touched by the beauty. No matter how hard I tried to ignore it, it made my soul smile.

We passed 'The Eagle Tavern' that was situated amongst these hills and trees, and Bill suddenly perked up again, 'Great place that. Really nice ales,' he said, trying to convince me to snap out of my determined, miserable state and pull over; but I wasn't having it.

'Sounds great,' I said as we whizzed past; and that's pretty much how the rest of the road trip went. Skipping the 'East Devon Area of Natural Beauty' and joining the A30 where the A303 suddenly diminished, seamlessly.

We sped past Honiton and continued down the A30 until we joined up with the M5. Which would take us south a little until we crossed the River Exe and rejoin the A30 on the other side.

We cut back up north after connecting to the A road, skipping Exeter and heading towards Ide. Almost immediately, Bill's voice bellowed, like a drill sergeant in the army. 'Come off here!'

I jumped in my seat, 'No, we can be in Par by tonight if we continue like this.'

'Alex, turn off right now. For cryin' out loud, snap out of it and grow a pair. Shit happens, that's life; but if you're gonna let one incident affect you like this then you're in for a very miserable life. Turn off and at least drive through Dartmoor. I'm not saying you have to stop off anywhere, but do yourself a favour and get off the A30 and drive through the national park.'

There was an awkward silence, that seemed to go on forever. I knew he was right, but I was also very proud and stubborn. Suddenly I felt a liquid hit me and shake me. Uncle Bill had tipped his tumbler over me, 'Turn! Now!'

'Fine!'

I indicated and came off the A30 and eventually found myself on 'Longdown Road' leading to 'Dartmoor National Park'. Immediately I felt my spirit lift, and I was secretly thankful to Bill for making me turn off.

The sky was bright blue, with hardly a cloud in sight. The sun was warm, and for the first time since the incident, I played some music again. I began to allow myself to enjoy the cruise, as we drifted round bends and the sun gleamed through the leaves and the branches, that often loomed over the now tiny, slim country lane.

I was welcomed into the national park by two quaint, picturesque, white houses; that sat on the right side of the lane. 'Welcome to Dartmoor,' came Bill with a friendly smile, once again. I smiled back and felt my body relax, and sink into my seat.

Hills of dense trees were off in the distance, and we were quickly enveloped in a cloak of green. For twenty minutes I continued down the winding country lanes, taking in the fresh air, with just the hint of cow dung - which was natural out here in the fields - keeping me fresh.

Eventually, after negotiating a particularly tight corner, a small sign welcomed me into 'Moretonhampstead, Ancient Market Town.' I followed through, with yet another sharp bend to tackle before arriving in the charming village. The lanes became even tighter, and I found myself pulling up into the centre of the town. Tearooms, an Inn and

'Moreton House' all welcomed me, as I sat at a junction. Ahead of me were shops and a hotel. I squinted to read the roadsigns, but they were at an awkward angle; straight over it was.

Moreonhampstead got cuter the further I passed through. I continued to drive straight on until I found myself leaving Moretonhampstead behind and back into the national park.

Already, I was satisfied with having come here; and so I continued to drive through the national park with a smile on my face. In time I found myself approaching an extremely ancient looking wall, with a sign indicating that 'Bovey Castle' was ahead.

I looked back to Bill and he smiled, with an encouraging nod. I smiled and threw on my indicator, specifying I would be pulling in. It had a long road leading up to it, and I passed a couple of gardeners trimming the hedges and cutting the grass.

Eventually I pulled up, and was met by the most grandiose of buildings. It didn't particularly resemble a castle, more of a manor, or abbey, but it was impressive nevertheless. I parked up in a bay, when I noticed there were golf caddy's stationed outside, alongside Royces and Bentleys. I suddenly got a strange feeling, as I expected this to be a ruined castle, with tourists walking around.

I slowly got out of the van and headed inside. The reception was even grander than the outside and I was dumb struck. 'Can I help you, sir?' came a very eloquent and well spoken voice behind me. I turned and saw the receptionist looking at me enquiringly. His hair was slicked back and pressed down to his scalp. He had a pencil-thin black moustache, and wore a body hugging tuxedo. I walked over nervously.

'Uhm,' I stuttered, 'Do you do, like, uh- tours?' Immediately I felt ridiculous and the receptionists face confirmed my stupidity.

'I'm sorry?'

'Nothing.'

'Are you interested in booking a room, sir?' I let out an uncontrolled laugh, looking about the place once more.

'No thank you,' I finally said, before swivelling round and marching straight back out the door.

I hopped back in the van, amused at the ridiculousness and started the engine. 'It's a bloody hotel,' I exclaimed. I reversed out of the parking bay, and faced the long road that lead back out into the country lanes, when an old rusted red banger car whizzed up towards me; smoke belching from the exhaust.

'What the-' I started. The car screeched to a halt and out from the passenger seat leapt a familiar face.

'Alex!' cried Amy, with her red hair flailing in the wind. She was wearing her green parker jacket, and muddy Dr Martens.

'Amy?' I questioned myself before she came bounding up to my drivers window. I was so confused, and it took me a moment before I realised I had to unwind it. 'How'd you find me?'

'I've been waiting! Where you been?' she said in her gentle Welsh accent and slapping my arm. I was a little flummoxed. 'I saw your van pull in to Moretonhampstead and knew you'd be heading here; it is what we agreed after all,' she winked.

A young man stepped out of the red banger car and leaned against his opened door. 'Who's that?' I asked, unable to take my eyes from him.

Amy chuckled to herself, 'Don't be so jealous, Alex,' she said cheekily. 'Why'd you take off so fast after Solstice?'

And there it was. The question I had dreaded from the moment I left. 'I just felt awkward, thought it was for the best; besides, I didn't think you'd really be that concerned.'

She looked up at me, almost lovingly, and for a minute, there was nothing else in the world; just those big hazel eyes looking into mine. 'Well I was,' she said, sincerely.

She invited me back to Moretonhamptead, for a pint and to see the room she had taken up. I smiled, and looked back to the banger driver, who still stood behind his door, looking unimpressed.

'I have a better idea, jump in and come to Cornwall with me.'

She stood a moment, in thought, before a gentle smile crept across her face. 'I have to go back and grab my stuff. Let's grab a pint back at the inn, then we can go.'

We made our way back, the banger driver close behind, and bursting into the inn with high spirits. The banger driver didn't stay long, he said goodbye to Amy, collecting his own bags and then trundled off into the unknown; his modified exhaust disturbing everyone within earshot.

Eventually Amy came down from her room, bag in hand and smile across her face. I felt that darned butterfly feeling in my stomach again when I saw her glowing face approach me from across the room.

'Shall we get a pint for the road?' she asked sweetly.

'I've got something better,' I said, with a confident grin. I took her bag and walked her out to the van, which was parked up on the side of the street. I opened the sliding door, placed her bag next to mine, and showed her the optics in the wardrobe.

'Holy crap!' she yelled. I laughed and then pointed out the boxes of alcohol behind the sofa.

'Replace the Jack for me, and I'll get us started,' I said, climbing into the driver's seat, feeling warm, and strangely at home. I looked in the rear view mirror and saw Amy's backside perked in the air, as she leant over the sofa and reached down for a bottle. I smiled and started the engine, heading back to the road.

Chapter Nine

PAR

Before we knew it, we had silently crept into Par under nightfall. Amy and I had spent the remainder of the journey singing our hearts out, laughing and smiling, and she found the stories I told her about what I had been through since leaving her incredibly amusing.

We arrived onto Church Street from the hills westward. My heart warmed when I laid my eyes on the parish church, which was the welcoming sight I had been waiting for. I also felt a little sadness come over me; this was the first time I had been here since Bill's passing. I drove past with mixed feelings.

I drove us further up, and passed the beloved butchers, and the New Inn; a lively little pub that was always packed whenever I passed it. Uncle Bill had taken me to many live music events here, and I remembered us drunkenly staggering home one night, as Bill's bungalow was just at the top of the hill. I turned us onto Wells Street, before making another left turn onto Trenant Road.

Lights inside the various bungalows along Bill's road were mostly switched on, and I immediately felt at peace. The neighbours were friendly, and some of them were probably expecting my arrival at some point. I parked up on the drive way, and fumbled through my keys, as Amy came round to join me at the front door. Her arms wrapped around my waist, and she gripped me tightly from behind. 'This is nice,' she said.

I smiled, 'Wait until you see inside.' I finally found the key to the front door and let us both in. Once I stepped inside, all the memories of times shared with Bill came flooding back, and I found myself standing in the centre of the living room, cold, and looking around the now barren room, which had once been filled with an array of CDs, Vinyl records hung up on the walls, photos of an era long-gone, and little keepsakes Bill had kept hold of throughout his lifetime; now all gone.

There was, however, one black ornament I didn't recognise, sitting on the little table Bill kept next to his chair. I quickly walked over, confused and intrigued. There was a little sticky note attached, and I read it to myself.

'Rambo's ashes. You know what to do.'

'You okay?' asked Amy, sweetly.

'Yeah,' I replied, before explaining to Amy about Bill's wish to be mixed with his faithful dog's ashes. I tucked the sticky note into my pocket and looked around once more, 'It feels odd.' I felt a knot come into my throat, and my eyes felt decidedly damp. I swallowed, in an attempt to clear my throat and blinked a few times to avoid any tears. 'The room's through here. Let's get our bags in, and then there's something I want to show you.'

The night was growing old, and by the time Amy had laid our things down, and I had gone nostalgically through the bungalow, many of the homely lights throughout the neighbourhood had gone out. I walked Amy to the van, and as she sat patiently in the passenger's seat, I quickly opened the garage door, and stepped inside for a brief moment.

I had been collecting chunks of wood in preparation for what I was about to do, years in advance. I chucked the wood into the back of the camper - which took numerous trips - and plonked myself into the driver's seat.

I drove us back down the hill, but instead of turning right, back towards the church, I swung left; and headed up into the hills. The lane was tight, and hard to manoeuvre through. If there had been any oncoming vehicles it would have caused us trouble. Luckily, it was late for the folk around these parts and we made it over to the other side of the hill without hassle.

We arrived onto Par beach within four minutes of leaving the bungalow, as the beach literally sat on the other side of the hill. I parked us up and carried the heaps of wood onto the beach. I had taken countless walks along Par beach, pondering life's questions; before I had fallen into a miserable state of mind, and lost all excitement for such things. There was a public footpath up along the cliffs that I had discovered after a few visits, which connected to a few more remote beaches that not many knew about; I'd often taken my books and sat on the cliff's edge, reading and watching the soothing waves of the ocean's waters.

It was on an early walk, perhaps even my first, when I discovered a small patch of beach, separated from the main section of Par beach by a little stream, with a small metal bridge connecting the two. It even boasted a cave. When I found it, my intrigue and curiosity got the better of me - this was when they were at their peak - and I walked across the small bridge to investigate.

I found a small circular patch of burned grass, and my imagination was sparked. When I returned to the bungalow, Bill told me that in the summer, there were always beach fires and parties; from that moment on, I had always wanted to have myself a beach fire.

I threw the chunks of wood onto the sand, as Amy and I tucked ourselves up against the bottom of the cliffs. I got to setting up a beach fire. 'Yes!' I heard Amy say with excitement, as she reached into her deep pocketed parker and pulled out a flask. She whipped the top off and took a long gulp of whatever was inside.

She took out her phone, and soon 'Gimme Shelter - by The Rolling Stones' was echoing through the air. She began to spin in circles, arms out stretched; as she had done in the rain back in Amesbury - only this time it was under the pitch black darkness of the calming night; under stars so bright you'd think they glistened just for us. That's another thing I liked about being down in Cornwall, in London you'd see a couple stars at night and think yourself lucky, but here, here you could see whole galaxies!

I struggled to get any substantial flames to ignite the fire wood, and I grew more and more frustrated, as Amy continued to dance under the stars, the soft sounds of the waves ebbing and flowing. She finally looked over, probably confused as to why she couldn't yet feel the heat of the flames at the bottom of her legs. She laughed and bounded over. 'Here have some of this, it'll put hairs on your chest. At least, proper hairs, anyway,' she said, with a cheeky wink.

Before I knew it she had reached deep into another of her pockets and pulled out some kind of box, which turned out to be a fully fledged tinderbox.

I took a large gulp from Amy's flask and with a cough, 'Is there anything you don't keep in your pockets?'

'Fresh underwear,' she replied with a smirk.

I wasn't entirely sure whether I was disgusted or turned on. She got to her feet and walked over, swiping her flask back from me and taking a fresh sip. 'Doesn't mean I don't change them, they're just not in my pockets,' she said; my face must have given away my thoughts, 'Besides, usually I'm not wearing any.'

We danced around the flickering flames, listening to classic rock of the sixties and seventies; the very same ones Bill and I would have listened to. The pale full moon glistening above, reflecting off the ocean waves.

Eventually, we had tired ourselves out, and as the fresh sea salted air smacked our faces with slumbering effect, we laid our heads down onto the pale sand, Amy's tucked neatly into my neck, and we gazed up at the many stars twinkling above.

We laid together for hours. Discussing our lives up until this point. What we loved, what we loathed, and what we felt pretty indifferent to.

There was one particular question burning inside me that I had wanted to ask Amy back at Stonehenge; I just couldn't seem to find the right time. It could have been considered too intrusive, especially as I had only just met her and all; but I just felt there was something between Amy and I, like I had known her for years, and that no card was off the table.

'What are you running away from?' I finally asked. Neither of us looked to each other, instead we silently stared at the stars, like two lost fools.

There was a brief silence, though I could almost hear the cogs in Amy's head turning. 'Who says I'm running away from anything? Maybe I'm just having a good time,' she replied, finally. Her voice had dropped suddenly, and her usual cheerful, Welsh accent was nowhere to be seen; a faint hurt resonating from her words. I was silent, deciding it best not to pursue the matter any further; not right now anyway.

We continued to look up, wondering what was beyond our world - something I hadn't done for a long long time. Life's questions had evaded me, and I had lost all care for the goings on in the world, until now.

Amy and I continued to question into the early hours of the morning, until - side by side, embraced in each other's arms - we fell asleep, with smiles fixed upon our faces.

Out of nowhere I was forcibly shaken awake, with Amy screaming my name. 'Alex! The tide's coming in!' I quickly rubbed my eyes, and realised I was laying in a considerable amount of water, and shivering with cold! I leapt to my feet, as the tide thrashed at them.

I had to admit, I never realised the dangers of the changing tide; and it never entered my mind. Our belongings had already been swept away into the ocean, and before I knew it the water had already reached my shins. I took Amy by the hand and lead her up the little sanded island, across the bridge and up the beach to the parked van.

Amy and I - both shivering, drenched in bitterly cold water - raced to get back into the warmth of Bill's bungalow.

When we reached the safety, and welcome heat of Uncle Bill's, the first thing I did was track down towels. I looked up and down, and all over until I finally found some amongst the many stacked boxes in the spare room.

I handed one of the towels to Amy, and we both dabbed ourselves dry. 'Do you think I can have a shower?' Amy asked, looking up at me with those big eyes, mascara running down her face, still looking perfectly beautiful somehow.

'Of course,' I stuttered. I took her down the corridor, and showed her how the shower worked.

She went into the bedroom opposite and pulled a fresh t-shirt from her back pack. 'Thanks,' she said, as we looked at each other across the hallway, through opened doorways.

I went into the kitchen, which was situated next to the bathroom, and began making us both a late night coffee; of course there was no milk in the fridge, so Amy would have to have hers black. As the kettle popped off, having reached its boiling point, I heard Amy's voice coming from next door. She had begun singing to herself, though I wasn't aware of the song.

I leaned against the kitchen counter, listening to her intently. She wasn't an amazing singer, but to me it sounded so sweet and perfect. I smiled and took a sip of my coffee, as my heart began to beat faster and faster; her voice echoing through the wall. I just wanted to take hold of her in my arms.

Her voice went on singing, care free and at complete ease. I couldn't take it anymore, I had to be with her. I gently placed my coffee down next to hers, and made way for the bathroom. I stood outside the door for a few moments, nervous. 'Go for it, son. Be bold,' came Bill's voice from down the corridor. I turned and saw him sitting in his brown armchair, that he had constantly occupied when he had been alive. My eyes gleamed and I smiled. I took hold of the door handle and slowly lowered it, heart pounding against my chest.

As I gently pushed open the door, hot steam gushed out into the hallway. I flicked off the light switch, creating complete darkness. 'Oh, shit. Alex!' Amy cried out.

'It's me.'

'Oh,' she said, before complete silence. I took this as a green light; she hadn't screamed at me to get out yet, at least. I dropped my clothes to the floor and climbed into the shower. Impatiently I grasped her into my arms and kissed her passionately. We showered together, admiring each other's bodies and scrubbing each other clean. The smoothness of each other's wet skin; every bump and curve. The dimples in her lower back, running our fingers through each other's hair. We passionately kissed once more before finally heading to bed. Falling asleep in each other's arms peacefully.

The next few days we spent touring Cornwall together during the day; and in the evenings we would order takeaways and sift through Bill's vintage films. I introduced Amy to her first James Dean picture, like Bill had once done for me during that magical week.

Amy went crazy for Bill's vast collection of music, and we would often get drunk listening to our favourite songs; laying on the floor, pretending we were back in the seventies, on fierce psychedelics and letting the music transport us to other dimensions.

Chapter Ten

FAREWELL UNCLE BILL

The day of the funeral came, and I hadn't slept much the night before. My thoughts were occupied with memories of Bill and I; or a story of his I had thought long forgotten. The sun pierced into the room, and I decided that, as early as it was, I'd make a start to the day.

I gently threw the duvet off of me, and crept out of bed, trying desperately not to wake Amy - who slept naked beside me. I popped the kettle on and made my morning coffee, before slowly stepping into the living room. Up until this point, I had always sat on the sofa, not wanting to sit in Bill's seat, but today I did.

I sunk into it, crashing down into the very core of the chair - it had been worn away so much by Bill I nearly spilt my scalding hot coffee all over myself. Bill had a very large window next to his seat, that looked out over the hill, and I pulled open the blinds, staring into the early morning skies, and drinking my coffee as Uncle Bill would have done.

The neighbourhood was silent, eerily so, like a ghost town as I watched the many seagulls soaring above. I had spent a long time going through the vast amounts of mail that had been posted throughout the time Bill had died, and today was the only day I had been up early enough to catch the eager postlady.

I saw her approach the driveway, and then make her way to the door and its letterbox. Just as she had placed envelopes into the slip, and turned to walk away, I managed to swing open the front door, and call out. 'Excuse me! He, uh, he no longer lives at this address.'

The postlady smiled and collected the mail, before dutifully delivering to all the other doors down the road. I stood and watched her for a brief moment, wondering how she was unaware of Bill's passing. Everybody spoke to each other in Par, and I assumed it was common knowledge. I closed the door and made my way back into the living room; plonking myself back down into Bill's chair.

There were gentle thuds coming from the hallway, and when I turned to figure out where they were coming from, Amy's petite feet came bounding down, with my phone in her hand. She was wearing one of my tops, which draped over her, stopping mid thigh. There's something so warming about a girl wearing only your t-shirt.

'Your mum called,' she said, handing me my phone and gently placing herself on my lap. 'How you holdin' up?'

I didn't answer, just gently nodded my head. Everything felt surreal, like I was living in some sort of dream, and none of this was actually happening. Strangely I thought I'd feel more upset, more... affected. Perhaps I had psychologically numbed myself, or had been in anticipation for this moment for so long, I had already experienced this moment again and again.

I went into the kitchen and made us both another coffee, before putting together a small breakfast for us both. Nothing special, just toast and butter.

It was quiet between us - I guess Amy didn't want to say anything out of place.

After breakfast I slowly got to my feet and washed up our plates and mugs. Since being here, I had managed to rustle through almost all of Bill's boxes, and pulled out certain items of interest. Posters from the sixties and seventies - all of which were from events Bill had managed security for. Photographs from his times in Brentford, t-shirts, and all kinds of memorabilia.

Of course I had also sorted through his music collection, and had brought 'Peter Green's Fleetwood Mac' CD in from the camper. After I finished washing up, I put it into the record player, and let 'Albatross' wail out on repeat. For the first play over, I just stood in front of the speakers, keeping my eyes closed and remembering back to the day Bill played this to me for the first time. It was the first CD he ever played for me. Suddenly I felt my eyes fill up, the inside of my nose itched as I fought back the sudden tears; my throat tightened. It was almost as if Bill was talking to me through the music.

I opened my eyes as a tear fell down my cheek and I turned. My phone was vibrating, and Amy was sitting out in the front garden on the bench, smoking. I wiped away my tear and answered the phone. 'Hi Mum.'

'Hi sweetie, you alright?'

'Yeah.'

'We'll be at the crematorium in about an hour, o'right?'

'Yeah, okay. I'll be there. See you soon,' and I hung up. I took a deep breath, as the bright sunny summer's morning lit up the room, before heading to the bedroom to change. I knew that everyone would be wearing suits, and that Uncle Bill didn't go in for all that kind of thing, so I threw on my tight black jeans, a black shirt buttoned down from the third, and a pair of sunglasses, as my final tribute to Bill.

I was beginning to feel the effects, and realise the significance of the day, and I began to feel a little nauseous from it. I stood in front of the mirror, as my stomach began to churn ever so slightly, before taking a deep breath and heading back into the living room.

'I'll pick you up after, okay?' I said to Amy.

'Sure.'

Shaking my head I picked up the urn with Rambo's ashes, before heading out to the camper.

I sat myself down, and took another deep breath before starting the engine and making my way to the crematorium. A few of the residents on the road were out in their gardens, and waved me by; some of whom would be attending the funeral in an hour or so.

As I turned past the New Inn, I looked back to see Bill in his usual spot, 'Cor, I wouldn't mind one last pint in there,' he said. Immediately I felt my tears and let out an ironic laugh.

'I guess this is it then. 'Bout bloody time, too. My bones are aching like a good'n,' he said.

I was lost for words, and didn't really know what to say. 'I'll have one for you later.'

'Good lad,' he said; and for a good five minutes there was silence, as the camper drove down all the roads Bill had done for many years previous. It wasn't often Bill had nothing to say, at least not on this trip. I looked back to him regularly, as he took gulps of his Jack Daniels, staring out of the window. I guessed he was saying a last goodbye to all of his neighbours, and probably cursing at one or two of them too.

Eventually he looked at me and laughed, seeing my red, puffy eyes and streaming nose. 'Oi you! I haven't spent the last few nights sitting here to see you cry like a wuss,' he said jokingly, except his body gave him away; his voice cracked slightly, and I noticed a slight glaze come over his eyes. There was another brief silence, as we looked at one another.

'You know, I've learnt from you too. You're always saying how much you enjoy coming down to see me, but to be honest with you mate, I always look forward to having you. Honestly. You know me, I'm not a man to surround myself with people. I don't like 'em. I don't have many friends, and that's okay; but I'm always happy to see and speak with you Alex,' he said, looking out the window and never making eye contact. 'I'm not one for all this soppy mumbo jumbo, you know that,' he continued, embarrassed to look at me, 'You're going to do well in life mate, I'll make sure of it.'

I suddenly found myself pulling into the crematorium, and I could find no words. I knew how hard it was for Bill to express himself. He finally looked at me, 'I guess I'll see you in there.'

For the first time, I turned the rear view mirror onto myself so I could tidy up my red face. I wiped my eyes dry and cleared my throat. When I turned the mirror back to face the rear window, Bill had gone; for the final time.

I got out of the van, and greeted friends and family, including my mum, before we all made our way inside the crematorium.

***

After the hour-long service everyone streamed out of the thick wooden doors. Many people were crying, but I found I was able to keep composed throughout.

There were all types of people, I was the youngest to have had a personal relationship with Bill. 'That was a beautiful speech,' came Bill's daughter, who I had only ever heard of, but never met. 'It sounds like you had a good relationship with my father,' she continued.

'Yeah. He was a great man,' I replied.

'He sure was,' a little solemn, hanging her head slightly.

From what Bill had told me, they very rarely spoke, and I sensed in her tone a deep regret for that. She walked away with her husband and young daughter.

I caught a glimpse of an older man, about late sixties, walking through the crowd. He had on a leather vest, with a very famous motorcycle club's patch sewn to the back. I smiled and nodded to the man, who walked with a cane. Bill had told me all the stories of how he used to ride with this motorcycle 'club' - more commonly referred to as a gang - for many years, though he never allowed himself to officially join. He was good friends with the club's president, and I assumed that was who now rode away on the back of a roaring Harley.

Many people came up to me and congratulated me on a very moving speech, or wished me well. None of whom I'd ever met. My aunties, uncles and cousins all approached and asked me how I was coping of course, but more and more strangers approached, seemingly knowing me.

Finally, one approached with, 'That was lovely. I take it you're Alex? Bill spoke very highly of you.'

I was a little shocked. 'Thanks,' I said, suddenly trying to process what she had just said. I knew Bill and I had a good relationship, but I never took him for the type to say an awful lot; especially about me. My heart suddenly warmed, and I looked back at the empty camper van, sat silently and peacefully in the car park.

I walked over to a nearby bench and sat myself down, pulling out a Jack Daniels flask that I had found in one of Bill's boxes. I slowly unscrewed the lid, and took a sip of the fine bourbon whiskey I had filled it with earlier in the morning.

I observed the people that had congregated outside. Some were laughing and smiling, some melancholic and down. I wondered how Uncle Bill had touched all their lives; and if he had had such a profound impact on them, as he had me.

Eventually Mum cut across the courtyard and made her way over to me, smiling warmly. She sat herself down next to me, and waited a moment. 'Well done,' she said in a low whisper. I smiled. 'Are you coming back with us?' she asked, referring to her and my auntie, uncle and cousins. 'We'll have the ashes delivered in a couple of days, if you like,' as she wrapped an arm around me.

I took another sip from the flask, still looking at everyone in the courtyard. 'Actually, if you don't mind I think I'll stay here and collect the ashes in person; as soon as they're ready. Maybe stay in Par for a few more days.'

I could tell Mum was a little shocked, but supportive of the idea. 'Okay. I'll let them know you'd like to collect them personally.'

'Thank you.' She got up and kissed me on the forehead before heading back into the crematorium; eventually coming back out and encouraging everyone to move on to the wake. Just before she got in her car, she looked over to me with a smile, making sure I was okay. I lifted my flask and toasted, before she drove off.

I took the camper back to Bill's bungalow and collected Amy, and we picked up some lunch at the local Spar, before heading back to the crematorium. We sat in the car park for a few hours, enjoying a coffee or two whilst we waited for the ashes to be delivered.

Amy and I sat on the camper's side step and looked out at all the headstones and cremation sites that laid before us. 'Peaceful isn't it,' I said.

'Yeah.'

'It's insane how everything we work towards, and live for, just becomes nothing,' I uttered softly.

'I can't wait,' came Amy. I turned and looked at her, a little taken back. 'Not in a suicidal way or anything. I just look forward to the peace and quiet.'

I smiled and looked back amongst the headstones, remembering that Bill had said something very similar.

'Mr Stubbs?' came a voice from beside us. I looked over and saw a very friendly, elderly man standing in front of the van.

'Yes,' I said standing. The man was grasping a beautiful royal-red, marble urn; and he took a step towards me.

'Mr Stubbs, as specified we have placed your uncle's ashes within the urn you provided us with. Your mother informed us you would be waiting to collect his ashes today; if you could just follow me this way, we'll be able to get them signed off.' I nodded and smiled before following the man into a back entrance that sat tucked away from view.

I stepped into a compact room, that wasn't quite as presentable - to put it kindly - as the rooms I had been in up until this point. There was a large, thick oak table pushed up against the wall, with a wonderfully kind lady sat filing papers. She smiled at me and greeted me with a voice filled with compassion. I signed a few of her forms and presented my identification to prove I was indeed Alex Stubbs, before heading back out to Amy and the camper; with Bills ashes in hand.

'That's beautiful,' came Amy as she glanced over the urn. I had been the one to pick it out, as mum was stuck and Bill had already given me a rough idea of what he wanted before he died. We secured Bill's ashes onto the back seat next to Rambo's and started up the engine.

We started out down the narrow Cornish country lanes, and I suddenly realised there was one more thing I had to do for Bill. I quickly indicated left, and made my way back to Par.

I rushed back to the New Inn and parked up outside the entrance; throwing off my seatbelt and racing inside. 'What are you doing, Alex?' Amy asked, sticking her head out the window, but I just continued on.

'O'right there Alex?' came the thick Cornish accent of the bar owner, affectionately known as 'Skipper'. 'How you 'oldin' up?'

'I need two points of Guinness please Skipper,' I asked, with a great sense of pride in myself.

'Cumin' right up,' he replied joyfully, pouring the pints.

Skipper placed the Guinnesses down onto the counter, 'This one's on me lad, o'right.'

'Thank you, that one's for you. It was Bill's funeral today and I thought he would want one last pint with us.' Skipper smiled, and his eyes conveyed great empathy.

He took up his pint and raised it in the air, shouting 'To Bill!' The entire pub roared, toasting to my uncle.

'Wait,' I said, stopping Skipper from taking a glug. 'Bill's outside.'

'Ey?' Skipper replied, flummoxed.

I explained that I had Bill's ashes in the back of the camper, and lead Skipper out front. He laughed and patted me on the back, before we chugged on our Guinness's together, Skipper able to say his final farewell.

Amy and I drove a few miles to a cliff edge, that looked out over the setting sun. The sky was a deep orange and the sun was gradually lowering over the horizon. I looked in my rear view mirror, and all around out the windows to make sure nobody was around, before taking the van off road and parking it just before the cliff's edge.

Amy and I both got out of the van and stood hand in hand as the sky glowed a radiant bright orange. 'Ready?' she asked. I didn't reply immediately. Instead, for some bizarre reason, the image of Bill sitting on a fishing chair amongst the trees that night the camper had been stolen from me appeared in my mind. I laughed, and took out the letter Bill had sent to me via my Mum, the morning I left for my trip.

'Alex,

I'd like to take this time to let you know how I feel. You know I find it hard to express myself, but you should know that I think you're alright. It's been nice getting to know you, and even though it was later in life, we made the best of it. We're both very alike, you and me, you know that? But you're a man now, and you need to pull yourself together, alright? Stop moping about alone in your room, feeling sorry for yourself and day dreaming all the time. Go enjoy the world. You'll get no pity from me. If you want stories of your own then you need to venture out. Keep up the hard work with your acting, I reckon you've got what it takes. Get to America and say hi to Marilyn for me,

Bill.'

Tears ran down my cheek, and my throat knotted once again. I smiled to Amy and nodded. I solemnly returned to the camper; swinging open the side door I climbed into the back.

I gently removed the lid from both urns and, with very steady hands, I lifted Rambo and began pouring his ashes into Bill's; being vigilant not to pour any onto the seats. I watched, almost in slow motion, as the two souls where reunited once more.

Once all of Bill's favourite companion's ashes had mixed in with his I tightly sealed the now full red marble urn; looking at it a moment, imagining what the reunion might be like, smiling through the flowing tears.

I reached under the sink, and pulled out a wad of sticky notes from the cupboard; the same ones Bill had left around the camper. I ripped off a single note, and took out a pen, writing my own letter to Uncle Bill.

'*Thank you,*'

I folded the small piece of paper four times, before placing it inside the urn. I took up the now heavy ashes, and placed them down gently into the passenger's seat; locking it in place with the seatbelt.

The sun lowered rapidly, and the orange rays pierced through the windscreen, shining perfectly on Uncle Bill. I got out the van and walked around to the driver's door, before turning to Amy, 'Did you bring the brick?' I asked.

'Yeah, it's here,' she said, reaching into her large backpack and pulling out an old brick that Bill had lying around in his garage. She handed it to me and I jumped into the van, laying it on my lap.

I switched on the radio, and played Peter Green for Bill one last time, as I reversed back and stopped just before the road. I sat in park for a moment, as the gentle hum of the van vibrated through the air. I reached into my pocket and pulled out the flask with Jack Daniels poured into it. 'Until next time,' I said, toasting to Uncle Bill and taking a swig.

My heart pounded against my chest, and I took a deep breath, praying I would walk away from this with my life. I gently laid the brick onto the accelerator, and the van roared like a mighty lion as the revs screamed. I quickly released the parking break and Bills camper raced towards the cliff's edge. I threw her into second gear as we picked up speed, soaring closer and closer to the edge, before I swung open the door and leapt from inside.

I quickly got to my feet to see the light olive green Volkswagen camper speed off the cliff edge, gliding through the sky, before crashing down into the ocean's depths below. Just before it reached the edge, I'm sure I saw Bill on the back seat, looking out the window smiling, toasting his tumbler in one hand, and stroking his beloved Rambo in the other.

Amy joined me at my side, and she gently rested her head on my shoulder, as the final embers of the sun stretched above the horizon; the strawberry scent of her hair invading my nostrils. 'What are you going to do now?' she asked.

I looked out as the sun finally disappeared, and the sky began to darken. I thought for a moment, before looking down into her loving eyes, 'You tell me.'

ABOUT THE AUTHOR

Adam Gary was born on May 5th 1992, and raised in London, England. He is the son of Yvonne Richards and Darryl Gary. Adam's creative talents trace back to his mother - a dancer- and his great, great grand parents, a theatrical agent, and stage actress. Adam also shares his creative talents with a line of painters and writers on his father's side.

Adam first realised his interest in acting at the age of 6, and has gone on to perform in many various productions, and worked on major Hollywood blockbuster film sets. Adam is now a member of The National Youth Theatre of Great Britain, an exciting charity and theatre company that has nurtured some of the greatest British talent throughout the last sixty-one years.

At the time of publishing, Adam is extremely busy with his writing; working on the new television series, 'Nerdians' as well as his first full novel, 'The Adventures of Norgara and Lilithien' to be released side by side with the series.

Adam is also working on a new collection of poetry to raise awareness around depression, titled ';' in association with The Jermyn Street Theatre in London, and another collection of poems, 'Love Letters from the Heart and Soul' which is due for release in Febuary, 2018.

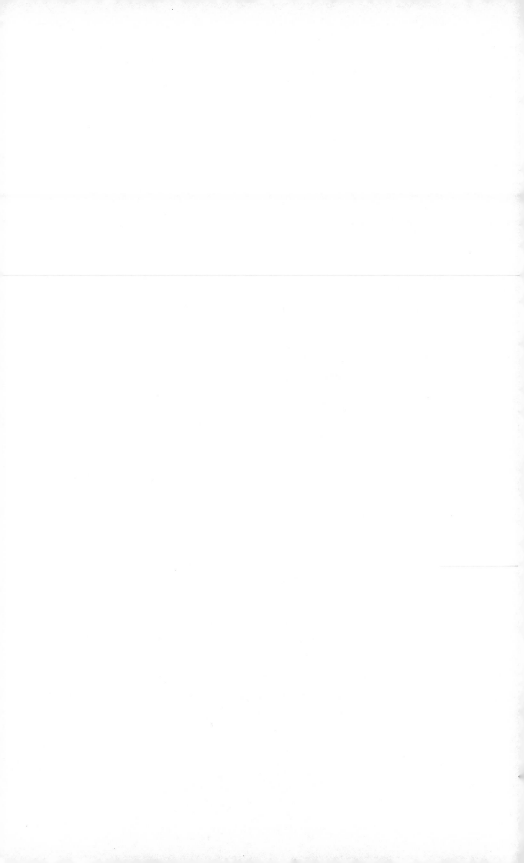

Lightning Source UK Ltd.
Milton Keynes UK
UKHW010608240719
346734UK00001B/439/P